O-Parts HUNTER

SEISHI KISHIMOTO

O-Parts Hunter

Spirit: A special energy force which only the O.P.T.s have. The amount of Spirit they have within them determines how strong of an O.P.T. they are.

O-Parts: Amazing artifacts with mystical powers left from an ancient civilization. They have been excavated from various ruins around the world. Depending on their Effects, O-Parts are given a rank from E to SS within a seven-tiered system.

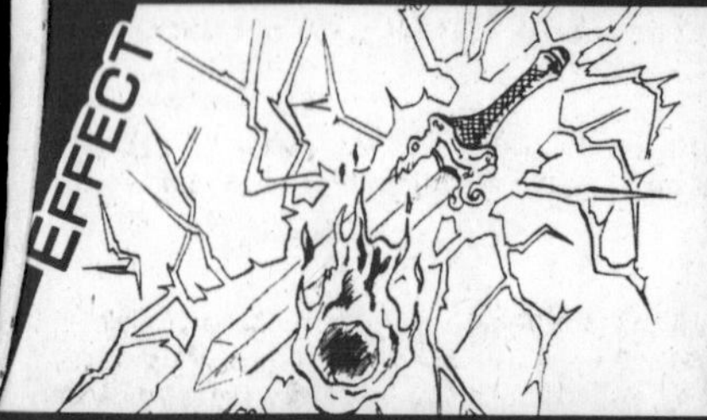

Effect: The special energy (power) the O-Parts possess. It can only be used when an O.P.T. sends his Spirit into an O-Part.

O.P.T.: One who has the ability to release and use the powers of the O-Parts. The name O.P.T. is an abbreviated form of O-Part Tactician.

CHARACTERS

Jio Freed
A wild O.P.T. boy whose dream is world domination! He has been emotionally damaged by his experiences in the past, but is still gung-ho about his new adventures! O-Part: New Zero-shiki (Rank B)
Effect: Triple (Increasing power by a factor of three)

Ruby
A treasure hunter who can decipher ancient texts. She meets Jio during her search for a legendary O-Part.

Satan
This demon is thought to be a mutated form of Jio. It is a creature shrouded in mystery with earth-shattering powers.

STORY

Ascald: a world where people fight amongst themselves in order to get their hands on mystical objects left behind by an ancient civilization...the O-Parts.

In that world, a monster that strikes fear into the hearts of the strongest of men is rumored to exist. Those who have seen the monster all tell of the same thing—that the number of the beast, 666, is engraved on its forehead.

***

Jio, an O.P.T. boy who wants to rule the world, travels the globe with Ball, a novice O.P.T., and Ruby, a girl searching for both her missing father and a legendary O-Part. On a quest to locate the Kabbalah ahead of the Stea Government and the Zenom Syndicate, Jio's team stumbles onto the sky city of Rock Bird, ruled by Ikaros, otherwise known as Beelzebub, a demon of the Kabbalah. Ikaros kidnaps Ruby in order to lure Jio into his clutches and so gain control of Satan, Jio's immensely powerful alter ego. But the scheme causes Jio's anger to erupt and bring destruction to Rock Bird and all of Ikaros's ambitions!

Table of Contents

CHAPTER 49 A FIERCE FIGHT

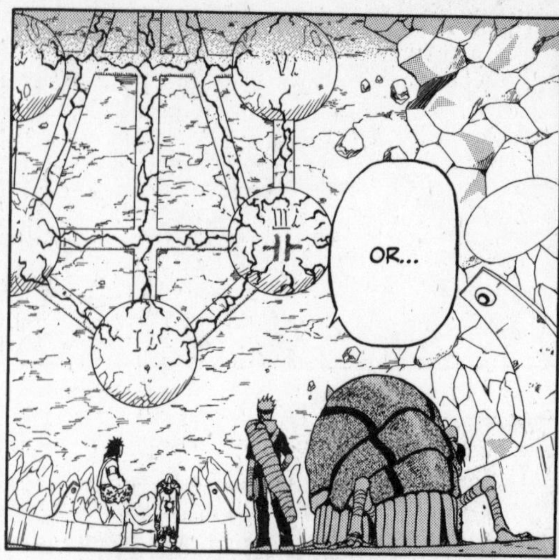
SO YOU WANNA DIS THE REST OF US...
...AND KISS UP TO OUR LEADER, HUH?
OR...

...IS THE DOG THINKING OF BITING HIS MASTER'S HAND?
GNAW

K-KUJAKU WOULDN'T D-DO SUCH A THING...
HE WOULD...
IT'S KUJAKU.

I'VE NO USE FOR YOU RIGHT NOW...

...SO BUG OFF.

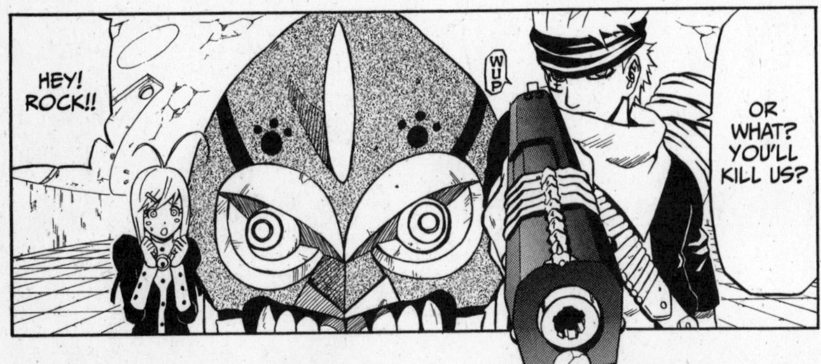
OR WHAT? YOU'LL KILL US?
WUP
HEY! ROCK!!

IF WE FIGHT HERE, NEITHER YOU NOR THE KABBALAH WILL REMAIN IN ONE PIECE.

WE WERE LISTENING, AND WE KNOW THERE'S STILL A RECIPE IN ROCK BIRD.
SO WE'LL BUG OFF, JUST LIKE YOU ASKED.
MASTER ZENOM WANTS US TO RETRIEVE IT.

TWTCH

WHZZZZZ
EH?

CRASH
SMASH

CLATTER
?!

KNK
IS EVERY-BODY ALL RIGHT?!
TNK
OWWW... Y-YO, I THINK I'M STILL ALIVE.

SO WHAT THE HELL WAS THAT?
I CAN MOVE NOW, ANYWAY.
WIGGLE
WIGGLE

!
KRKLE

LOOKS LIKE WE'RE THE ONLY ONES HERE.

CLUNK
ANNA !!

MALSE ...

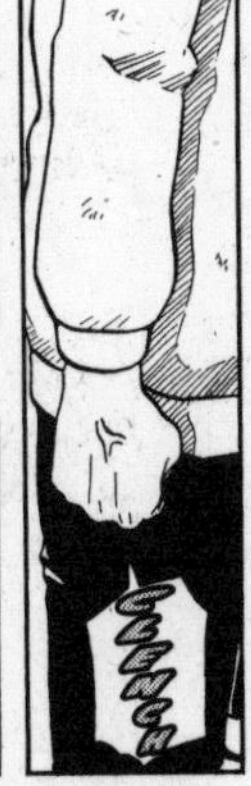
CLENCH

IKAROS ISN'T LIKE ANYONE WE'VE EVER FOUGHT...
HE'S TOO STRONG. EVEN JIO CAN'T...

WHEN IKAROS KILLED MALSE BEFORE MY EYES...
...

...I STOPPED CARING ABOUT ANYTHING.
FOR A SECOND I WANTED IKAROS TO KILL ME TOO...
BUT...

... JIO ISN'T JUST FIGHTING FOR RUBY...
...HE'S FIGHTING IKAROS... TO KEEP THE PROMISE HE MADE TO ME AS WELL.

SO I CAN'T DIE YET... I CAN'T *ALLOW* MYSELF TO DIE!!
I MUST LIVE FOR MALSE'S SAKE, AND TO GIVE JIO MY THANKS.

CLENCH
AFTER ALL...

...JIO WON'T LOSE AGAINST A GUY LIKE IKAROS!
I'M SURE OF IT.

YO, SHE'S RIGHT! WHAT WAS I THINKING?
I'M JIO'S FRIEND, I SHOULD BE MORE WILLING TO BELIEVE IN HIM...

...

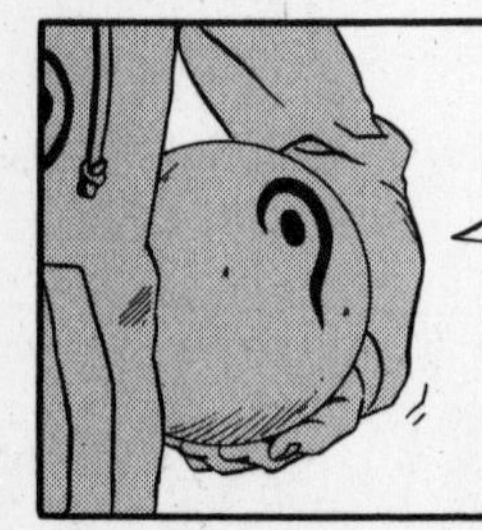
JIO CHANGED THINGS IN MY TOWN... SO I BET HE CAN DO THAT HERE, TOO...

AND HE'S STILL GOTTA DEFEAT THE GREAT AND POWERFUL ME!

...

CRASH

CRASH
CRASH
CRASH

WOOOOO

PANT
PANT
DAMN IT... SINCE HE TRANS-FORMED, HIS POWER AND SPEED HAVE IN-CREASED...
YOU'RE WORN OUT FROM USING SATAN'S POWER.
LET'S SEE HOW LONG YOU CAN DODGE...
PTUI
GWOOSH
...A FRAP MIND ATTACK IN THAT STATE!!
URGH! MY BODY FEELS HEAVY!!
WHFF
THWUMP

PANT
PANT

THE MOMENT THAT SPHERE GETS ME...
...IKAROS WILL BE ABLE TO CONTROL MY EVERY MOVEMENT.

I CAN'T MOVE !!
KILL ...
...THIS MAN.
NICE TO MEET YOU...
ZWING
HE MUST'VE USED IT THAT TIME, TOO.
SUH

BUT IF HE CAN ONLY CONTROL WHAT HE CAN SEE, I GUESS HE CAN'T CONTROL THE HEART INSIDE THE BODY.

MY ABILITY PRETTY MUCH CONSISTS OF SPEWING OUT THE DATA INSIDE ME.
I'LL PROBA-BLY USE IT ALL UP SOME-DAY...

BUT YOU, SATAN, ARE DIF- FERENT IN EVERY WAY.
YOURS IS THE *ULTIMATE* POWER WITHIN THE REVERSE KABBALAH.
THAT'S WHY YOU'RE *SATAN.*

AND I WILL CLAIM YOU.

ANGELS POUR OUT THE DATA THAT MAINTAIN THIS WORLD...

...WHILE WE DEMONS ABSORB THAT DATA...
...AND DE- STROY IT.

IT'S ONLY A MATTER OF TIME BEFORE YOUR POWERS BECOME MINE!!
PTUI

SPROING
WHOA!!
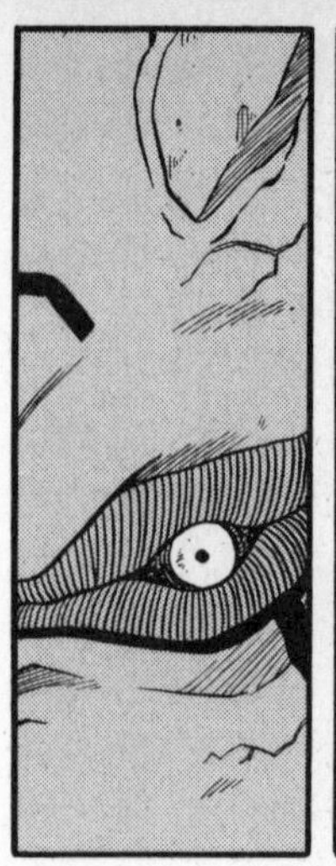

BLIT

IT'S THE FRAP MIND SPHERE HE SHOT AT ME BEFORE!!

SPWUT SPWUT

VOOOSH
TWOK TWOK
HAH!
TWOK

KRO
OOM

FLUP
SKSSSSH

!

GRIN

UH...

OOH ...

SPOING
AH!!

THE... THE DEVIL'S PAIN FORMULA'S VANISHED.
BUT HOW ...?

JIO!!!

!!

I... CAN'T MOVE...
GNNH

NOW, AT LAST, YOU SHALL...

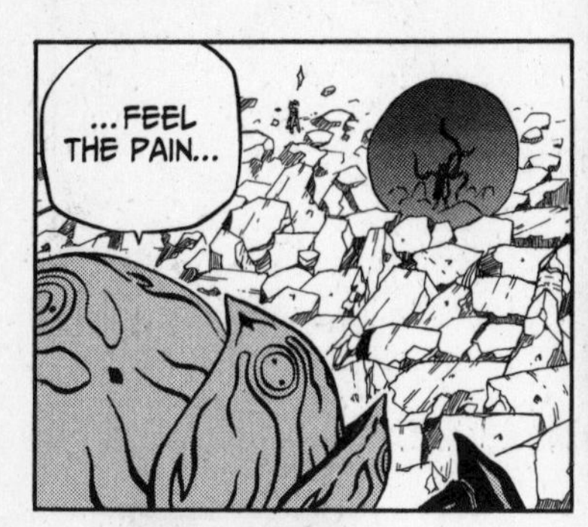
...FEEL THE PAIN...

...MY LITTLE PUPPET.

WAM
POOOM

GRUUH
CRACK
WHOP
YOU MAY AS WELL GIVE UP.
TRUP
HEH HEH HEH HEH... YOU'VE NO WINGS TO FLY, SATAN...
...SO YOU'RE HELP-LESS!
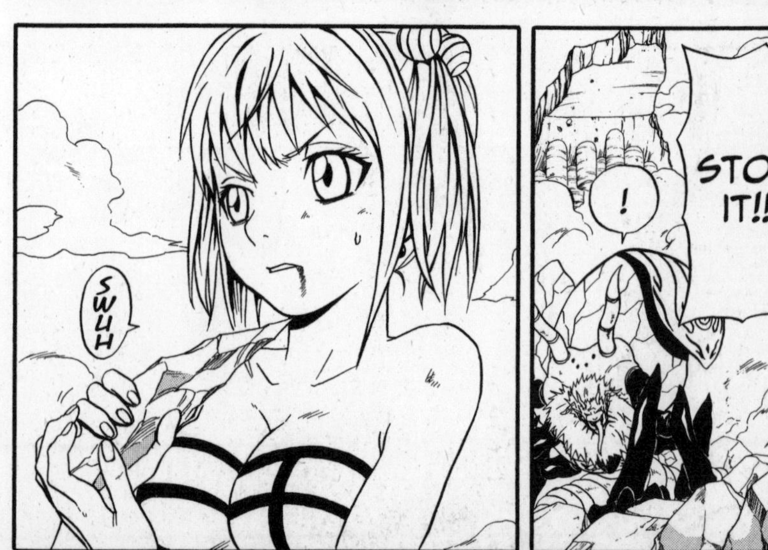
STOP IT!!
!
SWUH

WHAT'S THE MEANING OF THIS ...?
WITHOUT ME, YOU'RE NOT GOING TO BE ABLE TO...
... CONTROL SATAN'S POWERS!
PM
PM
NK

DON'T... DO THAT...
I'LL... DEFEAT ...
...RUBY ...

... IKAROS ...
...I PROMISE YOU.

STOP TALKING TOUGH, JIO!!

I...
CLENCH

TMP
...DON'T WANT YOU... TO HURT ANY-MORE ...
AH... AAH...

YOU'RE THE ONE WHO TAUGHT ME, RUBY.

I'LL NEVER GIVE UP OR RUN AWAY.

BUT...

BELIEVE IN ME!

...

BELIEVE IN YOUR BODY-GUARD...
...YOUR FRIEND!

BECOME YOUR FRIEND? NO WAY.
BUT I WON'T MIND BEING YOUR BODY-GUARD.

IT'S THE FIRST TIME...
...JIO SAID THAT TO MY FACE! ...

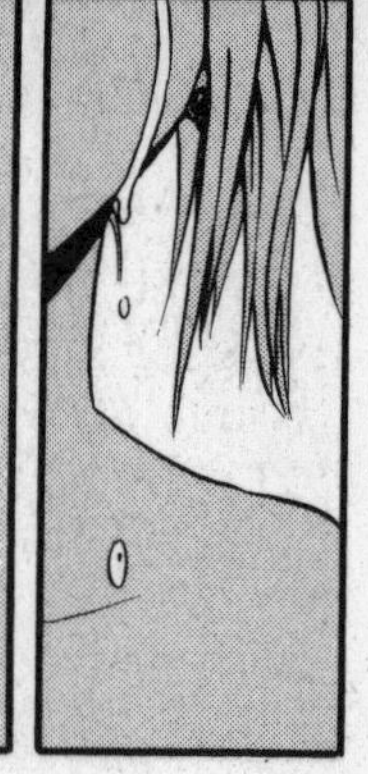
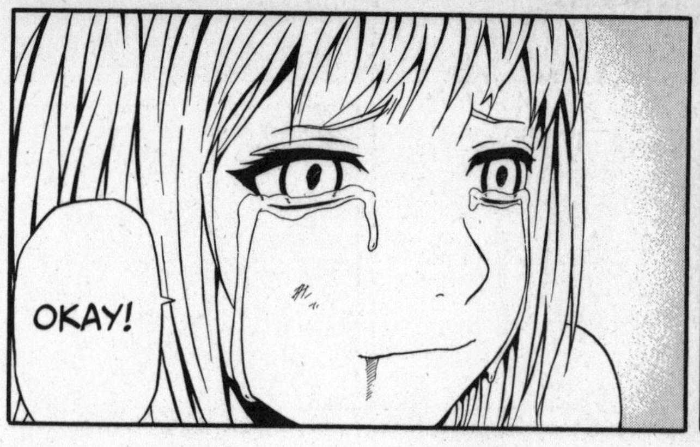
OKAY!

HEH HEH HEH HEH... YOU THINK YOU'LL DEFEAT ME?! TAKE A LOOK AT YOUR PRECIOUS RUBY!

FWUH
HUH?!

RUBY... NOW DO AS YOU'RE TOLD.
COME TO ME.

...

TUP

TUP
HEY! MY BODY'S MOVING ON ITS OWN!!
TUP

HEH HEH HEH ...
TM

I'M GOING TO PLACE THE DEVIL'S PAIN FORMULA INTO YOU AGAIN.

ZWUUU

WHAM
WHAM
WHAM
WHAM
WHAM
WHAM
?!

......BWINK
WHAT ?!

BWINK
AH!!

GOOD... I CAN MOVE.
WG
WG

FLUM

WHAT THE HELL HAP-PENED?!
KRK

I GOT BACK AT YOU. AND IT'S YOUR OWN FAULT FOR HAVING THOSE EXTRA ARMS.
SFF

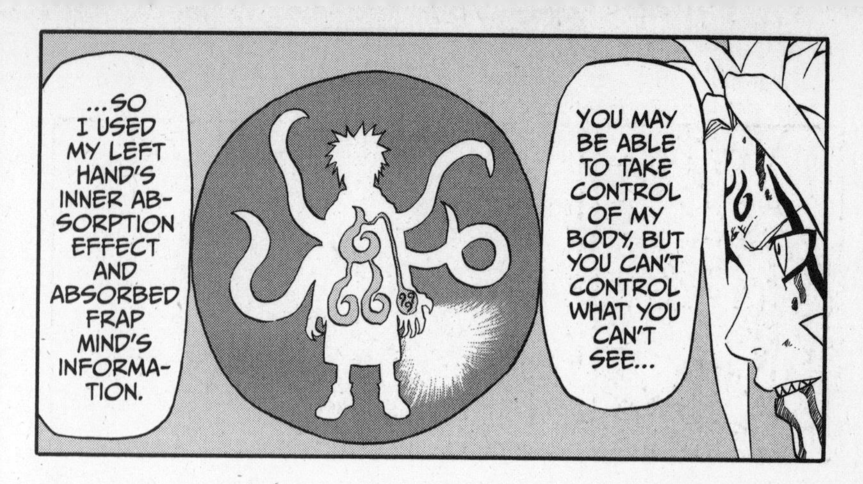
YOU MAY BE ABLE TO TAKE CONTROL OF MY BODY, BUT YOU CAN'T CONTROL WHAT YOU CAN'T SEE...
...SO I USED MY LEFT HAND'S INNER ABSORPTION EFFECT AND ABSORBED FRAP MIND'S INFORMATION.

URGH... YOU STILL SHOULDN'T HAVE BEEN ABLE TO USE IT AGAINST ME!
SO HOW DID YOU DO IT?!

WHEN WE WERE ALIGNED, I ADDED MY FRAP MIND SPACE...
...TO RUBY'S. YOU JUST DIDN'T SEE IT.
VP

I KNEW YOU'D SET YOUR EYES ON RUBY AGAIN...
...SO I WAS READY FOR IT.

I MOVED THE SPHERE ONTO YOU ONCE SHE GOT NEAR ENOUGH.
YOU DIDN'T CONSIDER THE POSSIBILITY OF A SURPRISE ATTACK FROM SUCH CLOSE QUARTERS, DID YOU.
TM

FORGET IT...

!

I CAN'T...
...HOLD MYSELF BACK ANY-MORE...
KRK
KRK

KRUNK

SNAP
I'M DONE TRYING TO AC-QUIRE SATAN'S POW-ERS!!!
ALL I WANT TO DO IS KILL YOU WITH MY BARE HANDS!!!

FWOOSH

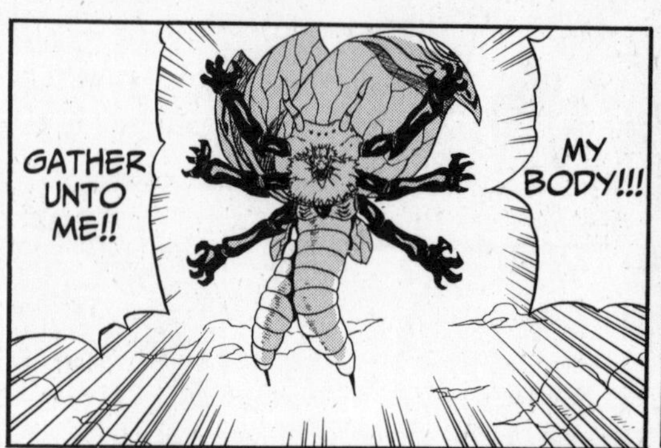
GATHER UNTO ME!!
MY BODY!!!

I CAN ONLY BELIEVE IN MYSELF, AFTER ALL.

SKREEE
RRRUMMMBLE

RUMBLE
WHAT IS THIS?!
?!

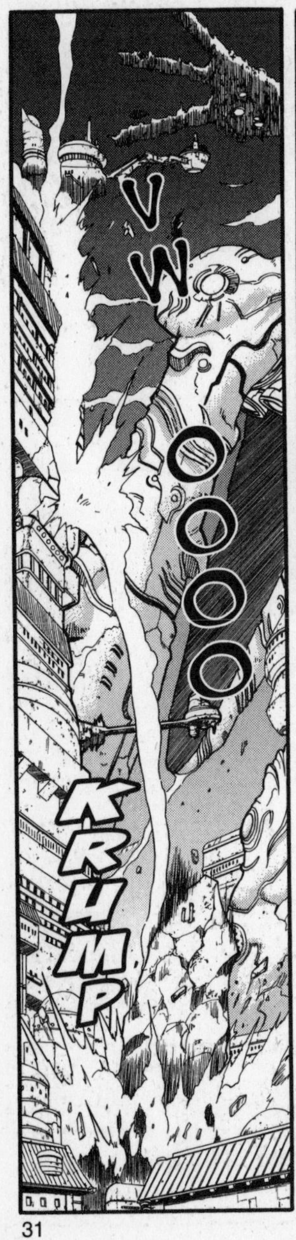
VWOOOOO
KRUMP

CRAACK
SKREEEEE

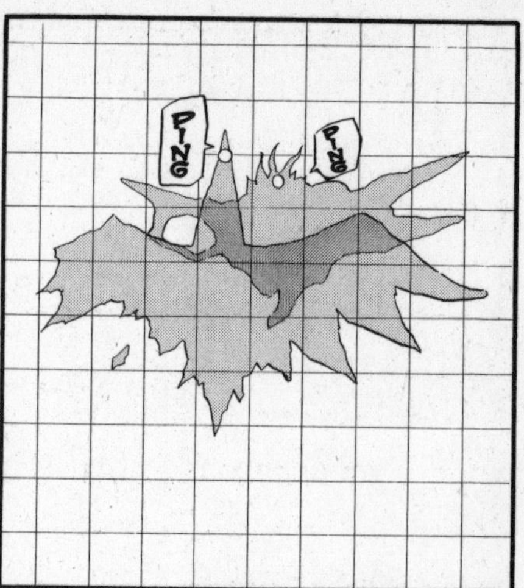
PING
PING

OH... MY GOD ...

WHAT'S WRONG?
WELL...
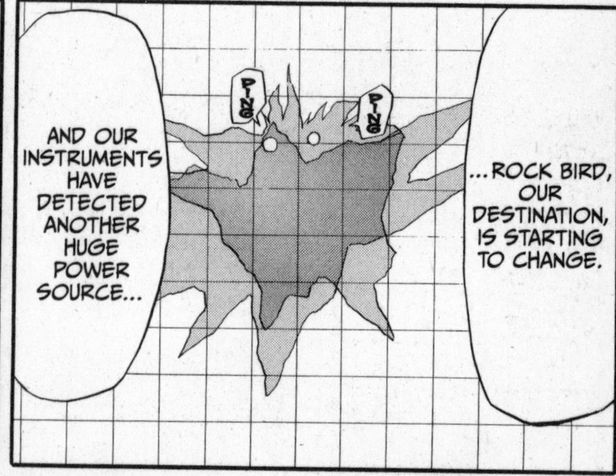
...ROCK BIRD, OUR DESTINATION, IS STARTING TO CHANGE.
PING
PING
AND OUR INSTRUMENTS HAVE DETECTED ANOTHER HUGE POWER SOURCE...

I CAN FEEL YOUR PRESENCE, SATAN...

AND SOON...
RANK SS O-PART
SHIN
VRRRRMM

SKREEE
EEEK!

YIKES! THE TOWN'S FALLING APART!!
WH-WHAT IS THAT?!

!!!!
RUMMMBLE

...

IT CAN'T BE...

THAT'S...

RUMB
RUMB
RUMB

IKAROS' REAL BODY WAS... THE CITY OF ROCK BIRD ITSELF?!!

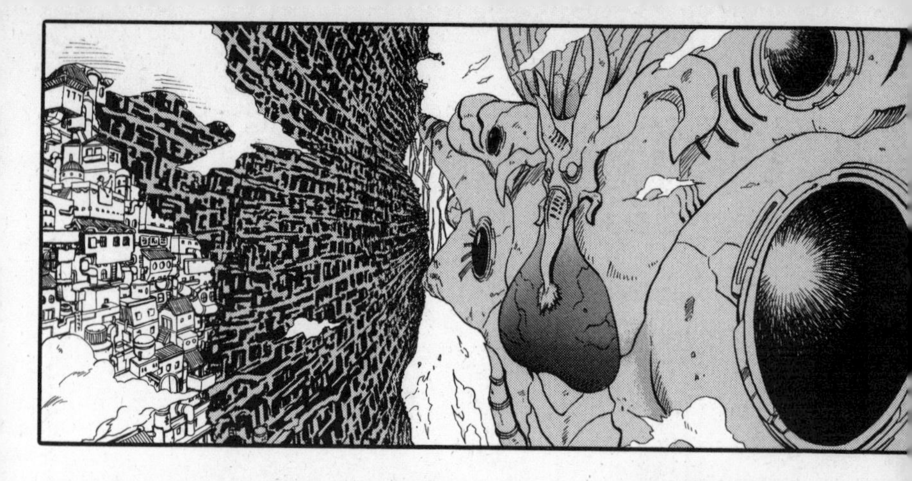

AAAARGH!
A MONS-TER'S EMERGED FROM THE CITY!!!
OH, LORD IKAROS... WE BESEECH THEE, PROTECT US FROM THIS ABOMINA-TION!!!

BLOOT

BY ALL THAT'S HOLY, THAT MONSTER IS IKAROS ...

I'LL OBLITERATE YOU ALONG WITH THE CITY THAT ENCASED MY BODY, JIO FREED.

RRRUMMBLE
HE'S REALLY PISSED.

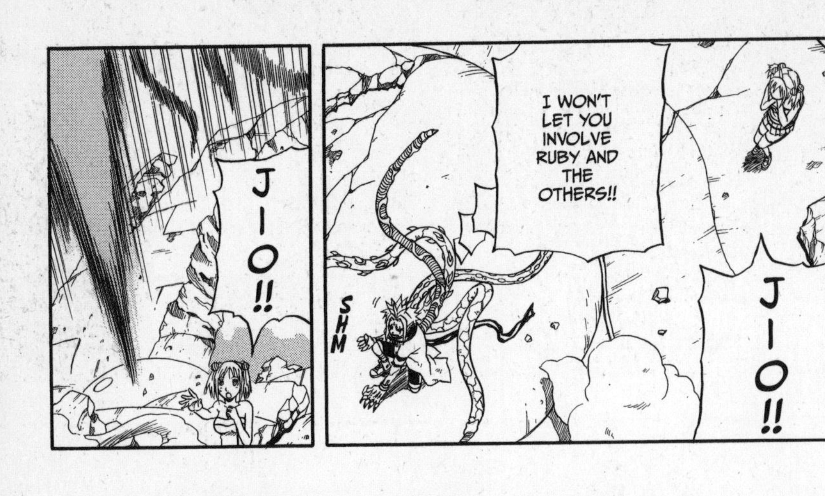
J I O!!
I WON'T LET YOU INVOLVE RUBY AND THE OTHERS!!
SHM
J I O!!

CRACKLE
SO WHO NEEDS WINGS?!
KA
RASH
AAAARGH!!!

ZIZZZ
BWAAM BWAAM BWAAM
BWAM
AAAAH!!!
PWFF
KASPLOOOSH

JIO!!!

BLUB BLUB BLUB

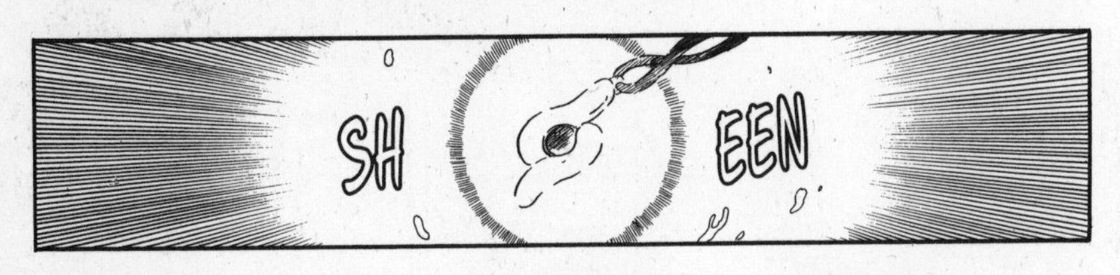
SH EEN

RUBY...

THIS IS...
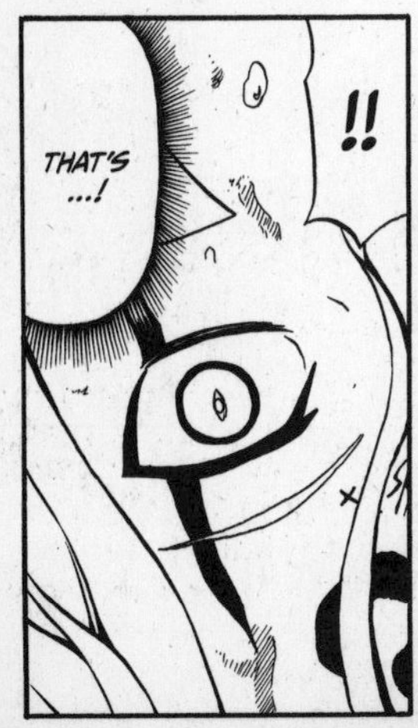
!!
THAT'S ...!

ACKLE
KA SMASH
SPLSH
WZZZ
SO THIS IS WHERE IT WENT.
MY ZERO-SHIKI!
BLUB BLUB
BET THAT MEANS...
I MUST BE INSIDE MALSE'S CAPSULE...

SKRAA

YO! I'VE GOT A REALLY BAD FEELING ABOUT THIS!

CAN EVERYBODY HEAR ME?!

!
HUH?

JIO...
WHAT'S THE MATTER, YOU TWO?
WIP
WIP
YO, IS THAT YOU, JIO? WHERE ARE YOU?!

I'M IN THE POD THAT WAS USED TO SPREAD MALSE'S SPIRIT OVER THE CITY...
...AND I'M USING MY SPIRIT TO CARRY MY VOICE TO YOU.

...

THE CITY'S FALLING APART AND A HUGE MONSTER'S APPEARED OUT OF IT!!
YEAH, I KNOW. THAT'S IKAROS' REAL BODY.
HE'S GOING TO BLOW THE WHOLE CITY APART.

THAT'S IKAROS?!

THAT'S IT, THEN. WE CAN'T DO ANYTHING AGAINST SUCH A CREATURE!
NO ONE CAN FIGHT HIM ALONE...

BLOB
...SO WE NEED TO JOIN FORCES.

YO, BUT HOW?

HEH HEH HEH...
SKRRRACKLE

LISTEN!
I NEED ALL OF YOU TO RELEASE YOUR SPIRIT...
...INTO THE GROUND RIGHT NOW!

INTO THE GROUND ...?
PAT

SOUNDS KIND OF CRAZY, BUT...
...IF IT'LL HELP SOME-HOW...
SHUUU

WE'LL DO THIS TOGETHER, MALSE...
PAT

WE'LL GIVE YOU ALL THE SPIRIT YOU NEED!
BRRRRRRUMMM
THANKS, EVERYONE.
SWUH

ABSORB!!
UUUUUUSH
THAT POD ENHANCES SPIRIT AND SENDS IT THROUGH-OUT THE CITY...
VRRROOOO
OH... WOW!!
I GET IT! JIO'S USING THE POD...
...TO ABSORB ALL THE SPIRIT IN TOWN!!

I HOPE MY MIND CAN STAND UP TO THIS!!
SHWOOOSH
DIE!!

CRAP! MY LEFT HAND'S GIVING WAY!!
KRK KRK
GLARE
SURRENDER TO ME, JIO, AND I'LL TAKE BEELZEBUB DOWN!
KRKLE KRKLE
!!

WHAT ARE YOU WORRIED ABOUT? I'M YOU.
KRKLE KRKLE

YOUR MIND BELONGS TO ME.
LET'S DESTROY IKAROS, THIS CITY, AND GO AWAY.
SLOOM
UNH... MY MIND IS...

GRIN

SHEEN
!

FOR... RUBY'S SAKE...

FOR EVERY-ONE'S SAKE...

I WON'T LOSE TO MYSELF, OR TO SATAN...
NOT IN A PLACE LIKE THIS...
SHM

I WON'T LOSE!!!
JIO!!!
SPLASH
HUH ?!

AN ANGEL ?!
YOU'RE GETTIN' A TASTE OF EVERYBODY'S SPIRIT.
INITIATE NEW ZERO-SHIKI'S TRIPLE EFFECT !!

OH... IT'S JIO!
AND HE'S... HE'S...
...STILL ABSORBING EVERYBODY'S SPIRIT.
I BET HE USES HIS SPECIAL MOVE...
SHUUUUU
SHUUUU

MARS IMPACT

CHAPTER 50 THE FINAL BLOW

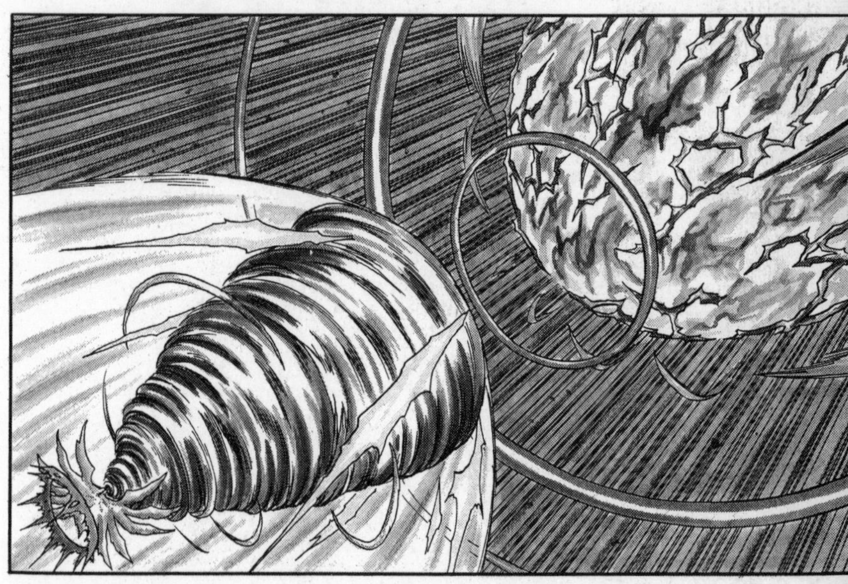

FLASH

DOM

KAW
KRNK
SKRNK
SKRNK
SKRN
SKRNK

EEEEE!
AAAGH!
JIO!!!
TSK!
AS I SAID, THE ONLY ONE I CAN TRULY TRUST IS MYSELF.
NOW THAT I'M IN MY TRUE FORM, YOU CANNOT BRING ME DOWN WITH A SINGLE BLOW...
...SO LONG AS YOU REFUSE TO USE SATAN'S POWERS.

...BUT I'M NOT FIGHTING YOU ON MY OWN!!

YOU'RE RIGHT...
SKRSH
SKRSH
SKRSH
SKRSH

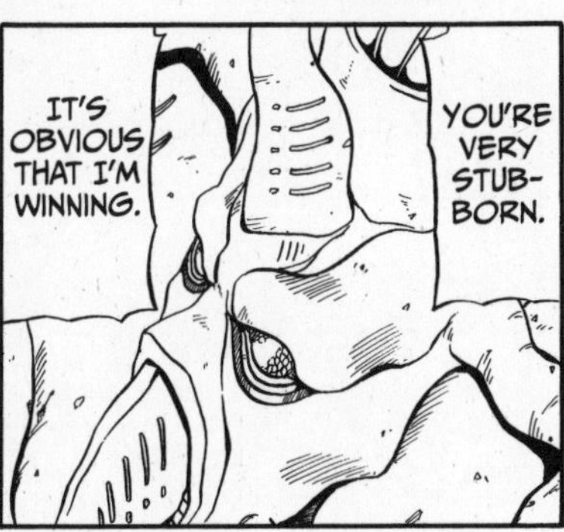
YOU'RE VERY STUB-BORN.
IT'S OBVIOUS THAT I'M WINNING.

OH YEAH? WELL...

SHUUUUU

I'LL WIN THIS TOURNAMENT SO I CAN MEET THAT IDIOT, IKAROS.
IT'S A PROM-ISE, ANNA!!

YOU'VE GOT TO HELP RUBY NO MATTER WHAT!!
YOU CAN DO IT, CAN'T YOU?
YOU CARE FOR HER THE MOST, RIGHT?

THIS IS... NOTHING ...
I CAN DEAL WITH THIS... WITH A SMILE...
SHUUUUUU

ZRRRRRRUMM
SHUU

...THAT'S YOUR OPIN-ION!!!

BRADOOOOM
MY ATTACK IS ON A DIFFERENT LEVEL FROM YOURS, IKAROS!
YOU IDIOT! I'LL VAPORIZE YOU!!
HRRAAGH!
IT'S NOT AN ATTACK OF ONE, BUT OF MANY!!!

HAARGH!

SATAN SHOULD NOT BE AWAKE IN HIM!! HOW HAS HE GAINED SUCH POWER?!

I...
I CAN'T MOVE!!
IMPOSSIBLE! HE'S PUSHING ME BACK!!!
TH... THAT'S ...12 WINGS

I'M—
FLASH
YAAARGH!!!
KRAKOOM

MY BODY ...
I'M A DEMON OF THE KABBALAH WITH A PERFECT BODY THAT'S FALLING APART...

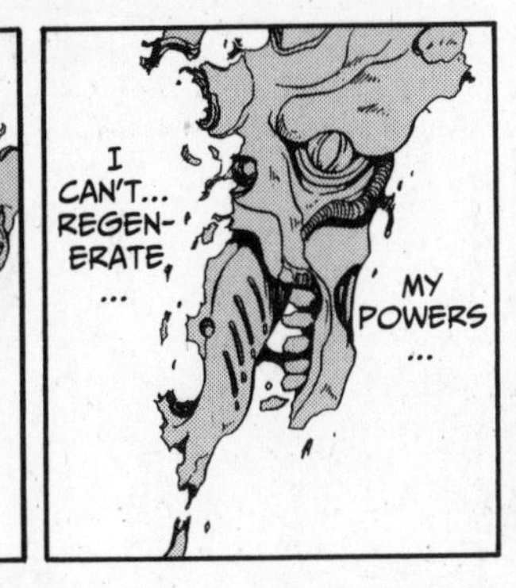
MY POWERS ...
I CAN'T... REGENERATE...

...MY... BO...DY ...

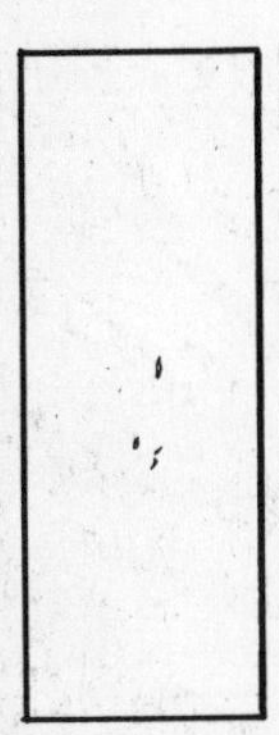

THE MONSTER'S VANISHED...
PHEW! 'BOUT TIME!
GURF

LET ME TELLYA, IF MY SILKY SKIN'S...
...BEEN DAMAGED, SOMEONE'S GONNA PAY!

!..
COULD JIO HAVE BEATEN IKAROS?
UH-HUH ...

I'D SAY HE'S DONE IT.

I BELIEVED IN YOU...
...JIO!

CRACK

WHAT?
THE RUKO ORE SHATTERED ...AND CHANGED INTO A RING!!
SO IT'S...
PFF
PFF

IT'S OVER, IKAROS, AND THIS TOWN...
CRUMBLE
CRACK
CRACK
THE PARTS PLASTERED WITH LIES ARE FALLING AWAY...

YO, WE GOTTA GET OUTTA HERE OR WE'RE DONE FOR!!
CRACK
BUT JIO AND THE OTHERS ARE STILL UP THERE...
CRUMBLE
CRACK

JIO WILL BE FINE. WE GOT THROUGH WORSE SITUATIONS, BELIEVE ME.
HE'LL HAVE NO TROU-BLE WITH THIS.

I'VE GOT ENOUGH FAITH IN HIM FOR BOTH OF US, ANNA.
!

...
HA HA... WELL SAID.

RIGHT, THEN! LET'S GO!!
OKAY!
BRRRUMBLE
FINALLY!

...ME.
PANT
PANT

PLEASE...

HELP ME... YOU'RE A CHOSEN ONE, AS AM I...
A *FRIEND* OF THE *SAME KABBALAH!* PLEASE...

A CHOSEN ONE, HUH?
I REALLY DON'T CARE ABOUT THAT...

NO, TRUST ME! WE'RE TWO OF A KIND!!
WHOOOOOOO

...BECAUSE YOU'LL NEVER KNOW WHAT A *FRIEND* IS...
...SINCE YOU ONLY BELIEVE IN YOURSELF.

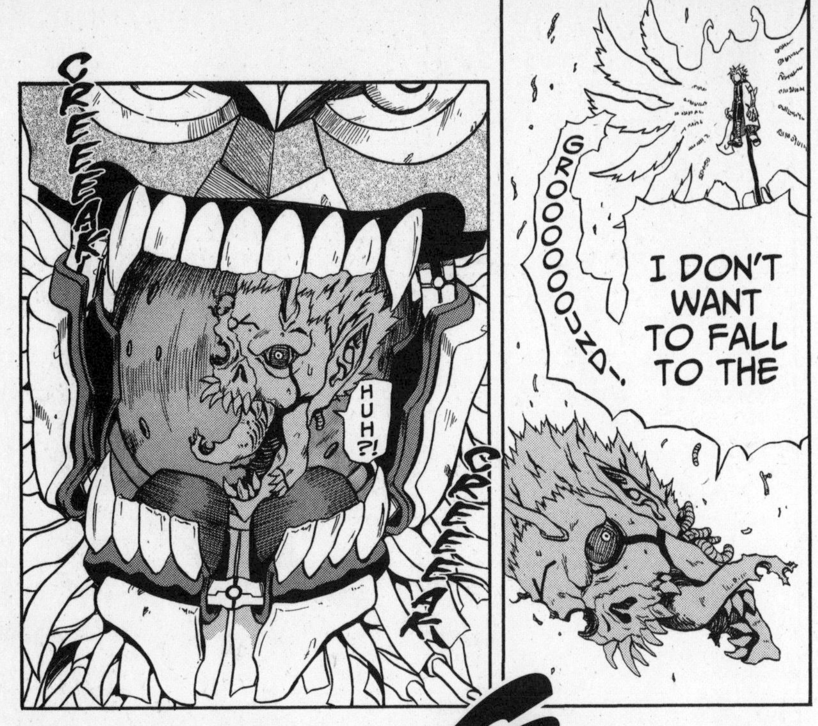
I DON'T WANT TO FALL TO THE
GROOOOOOUND!
CREEEAK
HUH?!
CREEEAK

SNAP

!

DON'T WORRY, YOU WON'T.

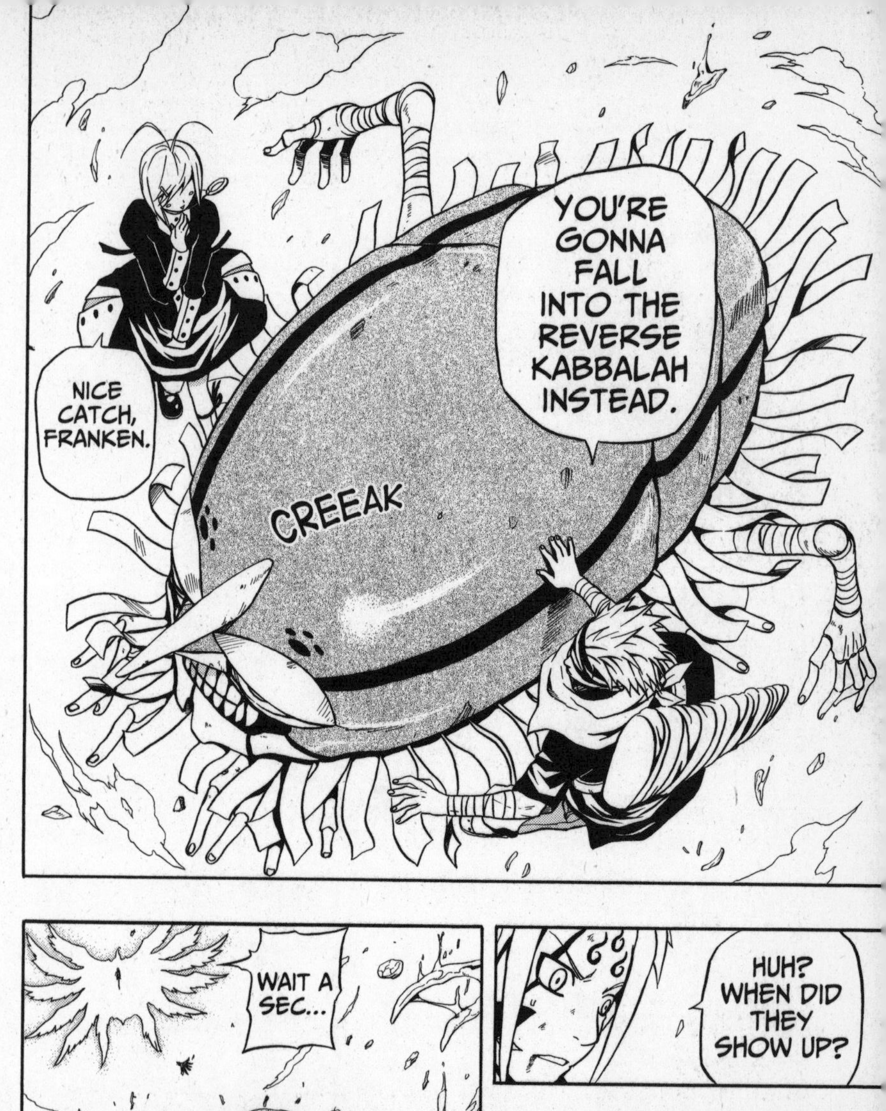

HUH? WHEN DID THEY SHOW UP?

...SOME TIME, SOME-WHERE...

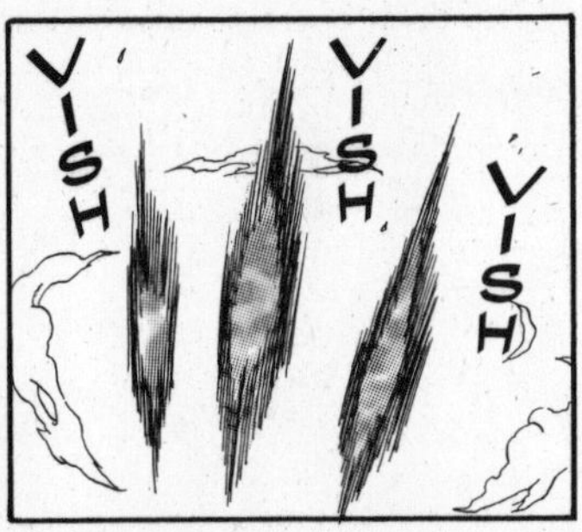
VISH
VISH
VISH

!

WHO WERE THEY...?

FWUUUU

THOOMP

PANT
FSSSSS
PANT

THROB
EESH...
EVERY-
BODY...
I...

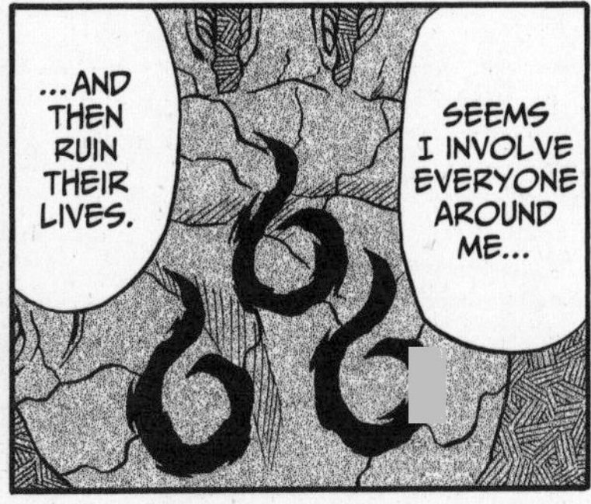
SEEMS I INVOLVE EVERYONE AROUND ME...
...AND THEN RUIN THEIR LIVES.

JIO...
KRUK
KRUM
KRUK
KRUM

YOU CAN'T BEAR THAT PAIN ALONE.

I WANT TO SHARE IT WITH YOU...
...IF YOU'LL LET ME.
BE-CAUSE... JIO, YOU'RE...

THEN...

GROOOP
GLOMM
...I'LL GIVE YOU PAIN.
JIO...

KRUK
KRUM
KRUK
KRUM

THE MONSTER VANISHED AND THE CITY'S...
...FALLING TO PIECES!
SAVE US, LORD IKAROS!

HUH?

AAAH! NO!
THE MONSTER! IT'S COMING BACK!

VRRRMMMM

DESTINATION CONFIRMED. WE'VE REACHED ROCK BIRD.
THAT THING IN FRONT OF US?
IT LOOKS AWFULLY ...DILAPIDATED.

VRRRMM

WHEN ONE OF THOSE HUGE OBJECTS ON OUR RADAR DISAPPEARED...
...ONE OF THE TWO RED ALERTS STOPPED, AS WELL.
PING

ONE OF THEM... DISAPPEARED?
BUT I CAN STILL FEEL HIM...
WHAT'S THE LOCATION OF THE REMAINING OBJECT?
SOMEWHERE AT THE TOP OF ROCK BIRD.

SATAN'S RIGHT IN FRONT OF ME...
I'M GOING IN ALONE.
OPEN THE BOW HATCH.

IS THAT WISE, SIR? I KNOW YOU LIKE TO FLY SOLO...
...BUT WE'RE TALKING ABOUT A RED ALERT. WHO KNOWS WHAT MAY HAPPEN.
I'M AWARE OF THAT.

THEN IF ANY-THING SHOULD HAPPEN ...
...I'LL BE READY TO ASSIST YOU...WITH SHIN...

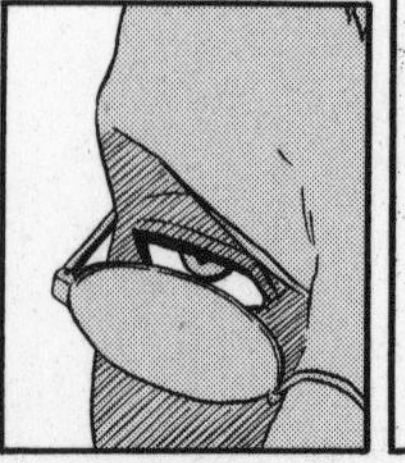

YOU WON'T NEED TO DO THAT.

SATAN... I'LL GET RID OF HIM...

...WITH MY OWN TWO HANDS!!
TROOP

JIO...

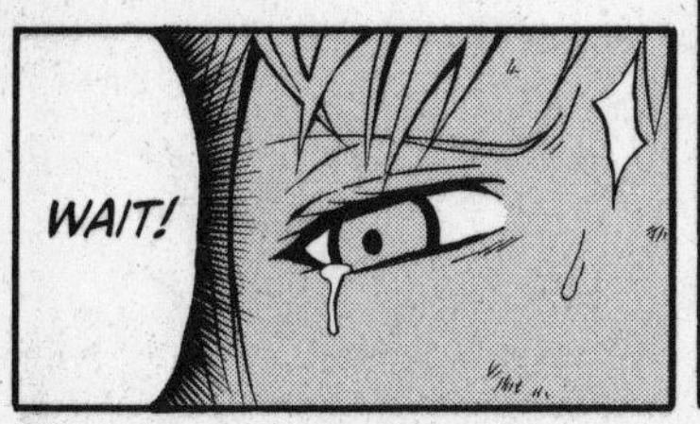
WAIT!

SO SHE WAS...TALKING ABOUT SATAN!

JIO MADE A DEAL WITH ME, AND CONTINUED TO USE THIS LEFT HAND.
SQUEEZE
THE MARK OF 666 IS MYSELF, SO THE MORE HE USES ITS POWER THE STRONGER MY MIND GETS AND THE WEAKER HIS BECOMES.

HE'S ALREADY CROSSED THE LINE.

THAT PENDANT WAS A PROBLEM, BUT NOW...

...THERE'S NO CHANCE THAT JIO'S MIND...
...WILL EVER RETURN.

A LIE...
GRAB

THAT'S A LIE!!!

HEH HEH... IT'S YOUR FAULT, RUBY...
SWUH

JIO USED HIS LEFT HAND...
...TO PROTECT YOU!
HEH HEH...

YOU'LL NEVER BE ABLE TO SHARE JIO'S PAIN.
HE'S ALONE, COMPLETELY ALONE.

SO, RUBY, YOUR EXISTENCE WAS NOTHING...
...BUT A NUISANCE AFTER ALL.

AND...

...TO YOUR...
...FATHER AS WELL!

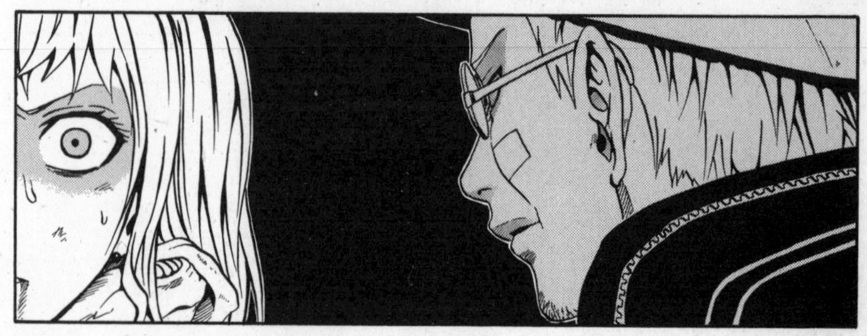

DO YOU SERIOUSLY BELIEVE A REAL FATHER WOULD...
...LEAVE HIS DAUGHTER AS HE DID? HEH HEH...
!

YOU WON'T ARGUE WITH ME?

STOP IT...

OW...
OW...

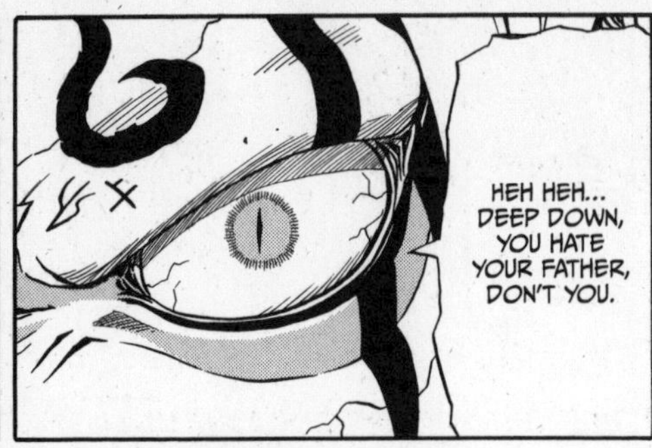
HEH HEH... DEEP DOWN, YOU HATE YOUR FATHER, DON'T YOU.

TUMP

KLAK

STOP IT!!!

THE HATRED INSIDE YOU IS WONDERFUL. YOU'VE DEVELOPED WELL.

C... CROSS!!
WHY ARE YOU HERE?!
SHMPH

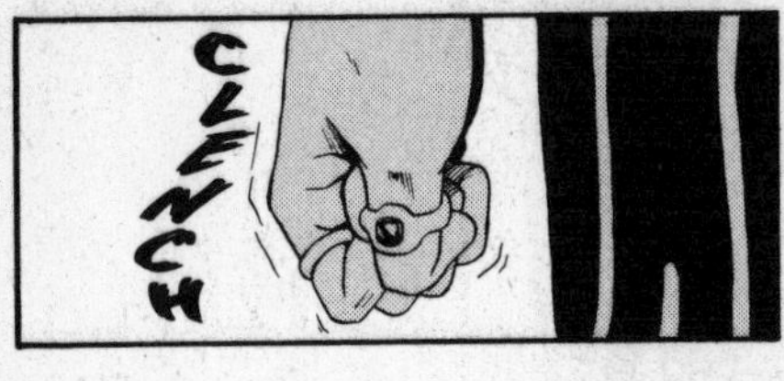
CLENCH

SO IT'S YOU, JIO FREED. I SHOULD'VE KNOWN.

LET ME SEE... THE LAST TIME I MET YOU WAS...

...WHEN I KILLED YOUR SISTER...
...AT THAT CHURCH.
HEH HEH HEH...

OH!
AH, HE'S A KID.
OH, I'M SORRY. I TOOK THE LIBERTY...
...OF SPENDING THE NIGHT HERE.
WHAT?
THEN YOU TWO ARE...
I BET WE'LL GET ALONG.
WE'LL PROBABLY BE ABLE TO BECOME GOOD FRIENDS.
I... I SHOULD GET GOING.
STP
OH, YOU'RE GOING ALREADY?
WELL THEN, HERE'S TO BOTH OF US GETTING STRONGER IN THE FUTURE.
I HOPE WE'LL MEET AGAIN SOME-DAY.

FLAP
IT'S A NICE DAY TODAY.
THROB
URGH!
I'VE FOUND IT...
OOOH... WHAT A PRETTY FLOWER.
LILY, I'M GOING AHEAD OF YOU.
TP TP
I'LL REPLANT IT BACK HOME.
UH-HUH.
THANKS.
COME TO THINK OF IT, I TOLD HIM WE'D MEET EACH OTHER AGAIN SOME-DAY...
...BUT I FORGOT TO ASK HIS NAME...
WAIT FOR ME, BIG BROTHER.
OH WELL.
I'M GOING TO LEAVE YOU IF YOU DON'T HURRY UP!

BIG BROTHER, LOOK!!

I'VE FOUND IT.
THE GREATEST DIAMOND IN THE ROUGH...

LONELINESS, HATRED, VENGEANCE...
BRR
I'M GOING TO PLANT THEM WITHIN YOU.
RMMBB!!

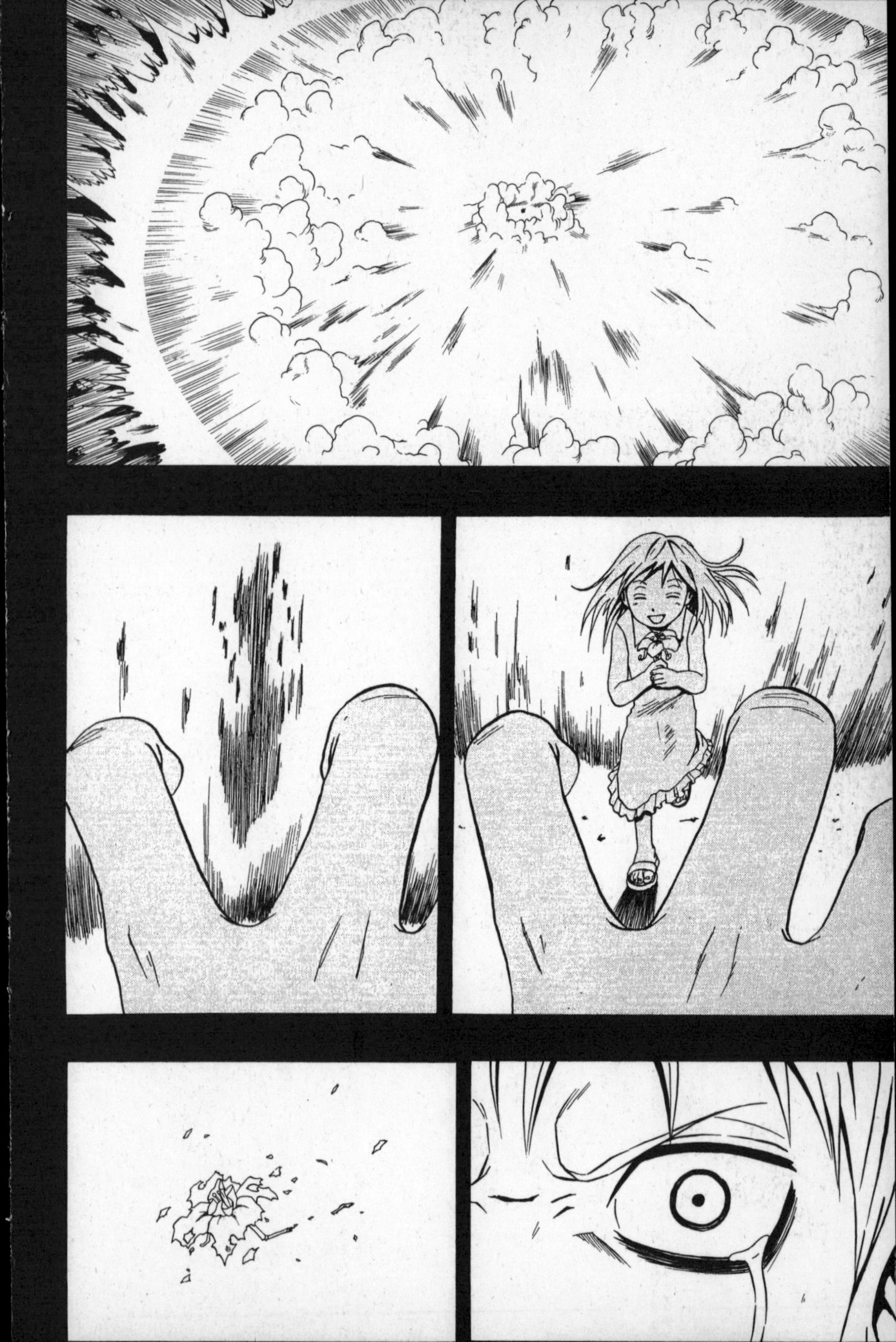

AS LONG AS YOU'RE WITH ME, I DON'T NEED ANYTHING ELSE. SO HERE'S A LITTLE PEACE OFFERING.
TH... THIS IS YOUR TREASURE, LILY... ARE YOU SURE?
IT'S OKAY. YOU'RE...
...MY HERO, BIG BROTHER.

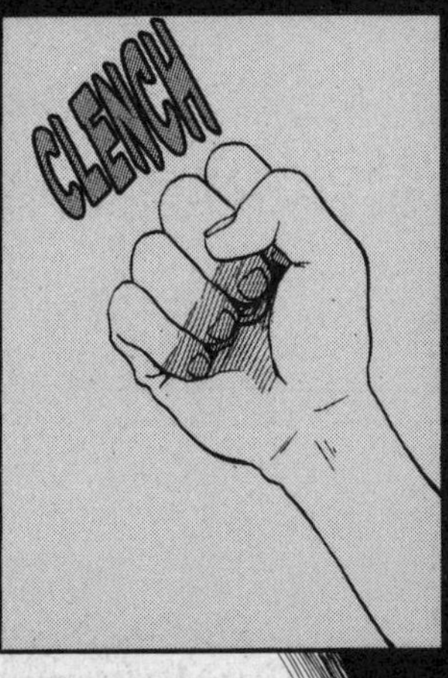
CLENCH

GRIIP
GRIIP
BLIB

SPLUP

SWUH
TIME FOR DIVINE JUSTICE...

...SATAN !!

CHAPTER 51 LIGHT AND DARK

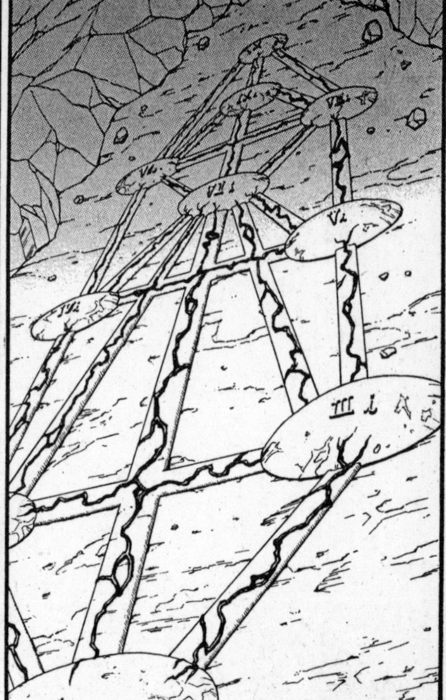

KZZ

CRACKLE
CRACKLE

FSSSSS

WE'RE BACK IN FRONT OF THE REVERSE KABBALAH. TIME TO SHOOT BEELZEBUB INSIDE.
SURE IS COLD OUTSIDE THE GLASS SPHERE.

HUH!
ZUP
B-BMP
B-BMP
B-BMP
ZWOOP
I DON'T LIKE THE LOOKS OF THIS, FRANKEN!
SPIT BEELZEBUB OUT IF YOU DON'T WANNA GET SUCKED INSIDE!!!

PTOO

SWOOOPP

?!

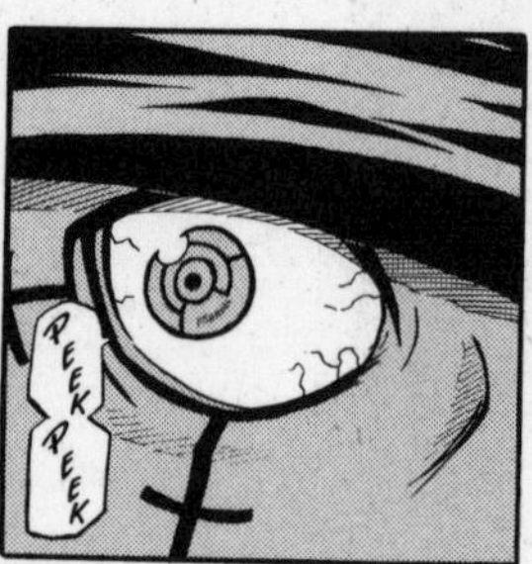
PEEK PEEK

THROB
URGH!

WHAT'S THE MATTER, ROCK?!
IT... IT'S... NOTHIN'...

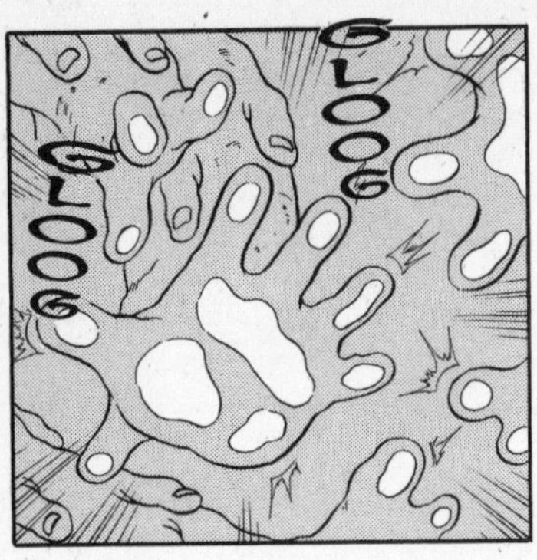
GLOOG
GLOOG

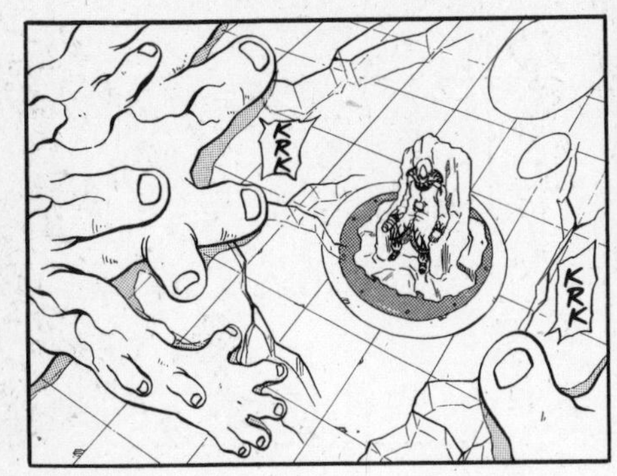
KRK
KRK

THE TENTACLES WANT TO SEIZE MASTER KUJAKU. AS I THOUGHT, HE'S...

...A DEMON OF THE REVERSE KABBALAH!!!

TWITCH

THE REVERSE KABBALAH WANTS TO CLAIM HIM.
WHICH SEPHIRAH IS...?

AH!

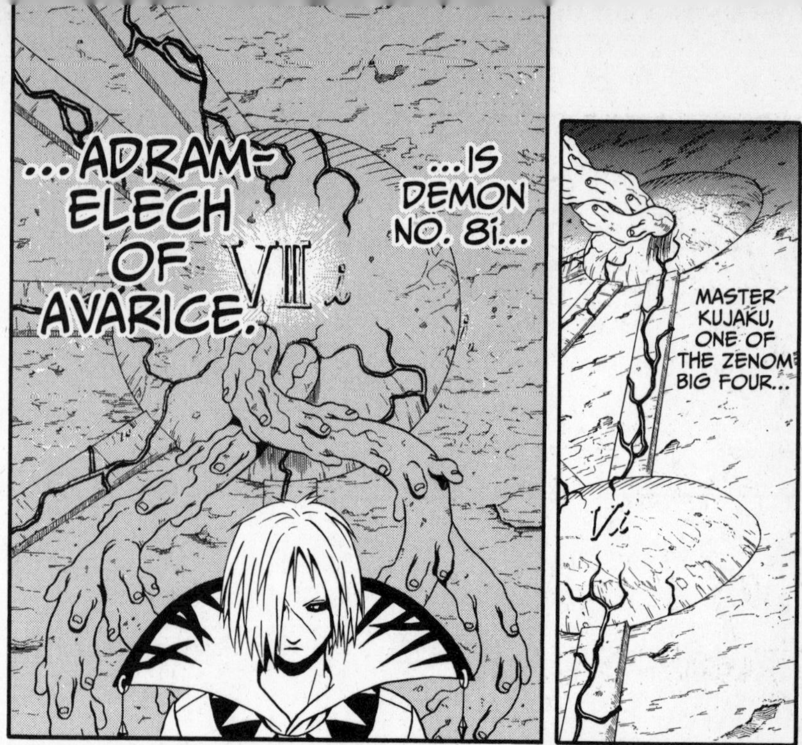
MASTER KUJAKU, ONE OF THE ZENOM BIG FOUR...
...IS DEMON NO. 8i...
...ADRAM-ELECH OF AVARICE.

KRICKLE

KUJAKU, YOU...

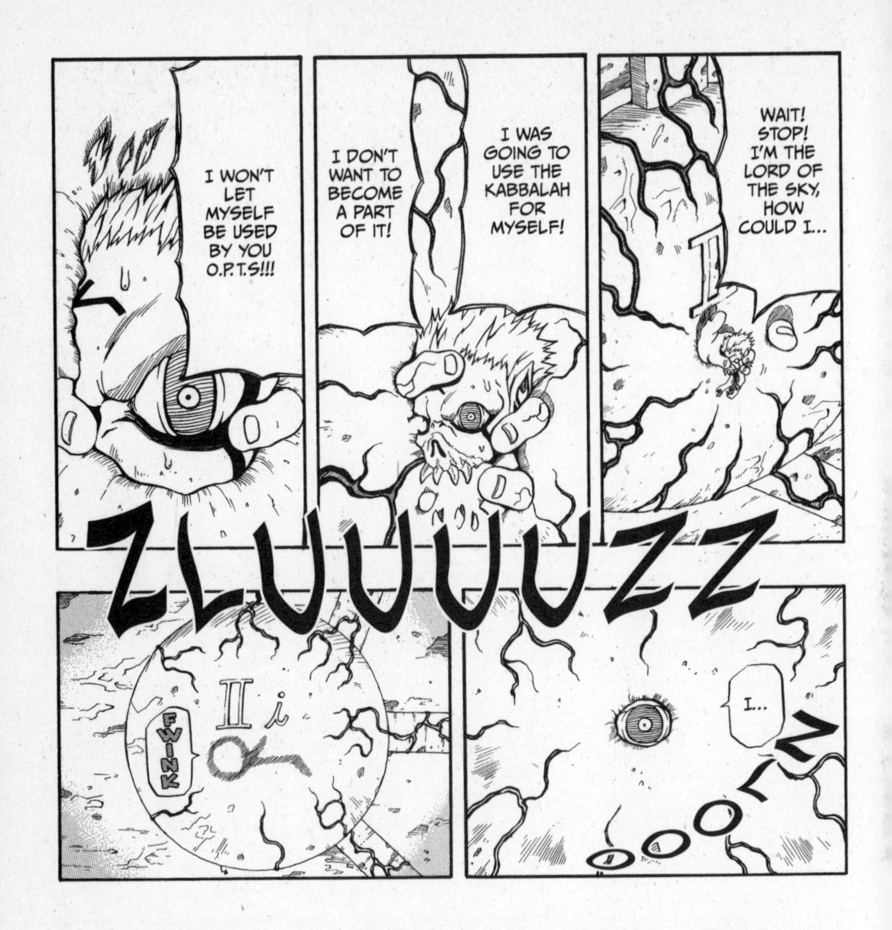
WAIT! STOP! I'M THE LORD OF THE SKY, HOW COULD I...
I WAS GOING TO USE THE KABBALAH FOR MYSELF!
I DON'T WANT TO BECOME A PART OF IT!
I WON'T LET MYSELF BE USED BY YOU O.P.T.S!!!
ZLUUUUUZZ
I...
ZLOOOO
FWINK
NO. 2i INANITY BEELZEBUB INSTALLATION COMPLETE

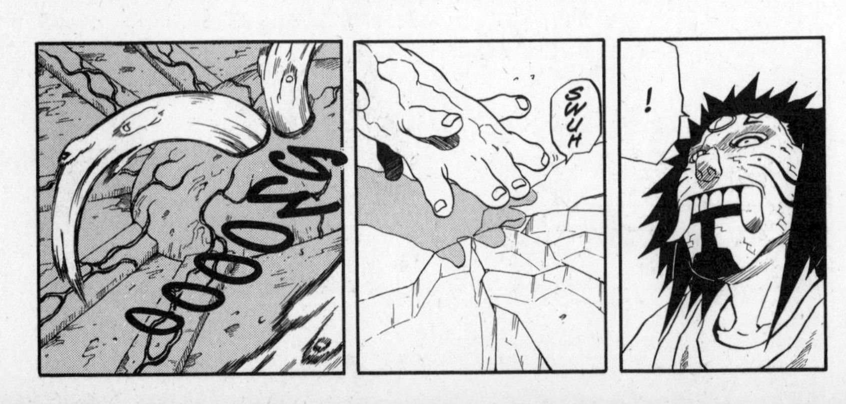
!
SWUH

B-BMP
B-BMP

LOOKS LIKE IT'S CALMED DOWN.
THANK GOD...

THE REVERSE KABBALAH MUST'VE BEEN STIMULATED BY THE INSTALLATION OF LUCIFUGE.
NOW THAT WE'VE INSTALLED BEELZEBUB, I HAVE TO THINK OF MASTER KUJAKU'S SAFETY, SO...
...I'LL HAVE HIM KEEP A SAFE DISTANCE FROM THE REVERSE KABBALAH THE NEXT TIME.

RRRUMM

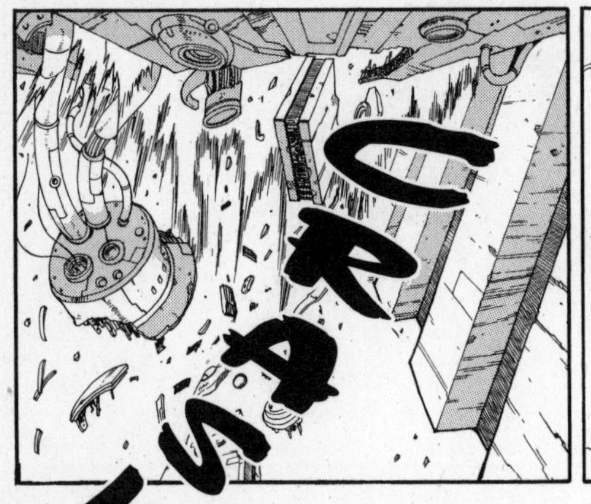
CRASH

WHOA!
AARGH!

TSK...

SNIFF
SNIFF

JAJA-MARU! WHERE'RE YOU GOING?! COME BACK!!
SPROING

POIT

VRRRMM

HOLDING ON TARGET AT 2000 METERS OFF THE BOW.
GOOD.

AS SOON AS SHIN'S LASER CANNON, ZOL, IS READY...

OPEN FIRE!

WHAT?
BUT THE COMMANDER IN CHIEF IS OVER THERE!!

EXACTLY. HE'S THERE, AND I'M HERE. TIME THAT KID...
...STEPPED ASIDE AND LEFT THE SERIOUS DECISION-MAKING TO THE ADULTS.

AS YOU CAN SEE, WE HAVE A RED ALERT OVER THERE.
PING
IF ANYTHING SHOULD HAPPEN, WE'LL BE IN TROUBLE AS WELL.

YOU'RE YOUNG, YOU DON'T WANT TO DIE YET, DO YOU?
UM... GUESS NOT...

WELL, DON'T WORRY.
WE'RE MEANT TO BE FLEXIBLE, AND ACT AS THE SITUATION WARRANTS.

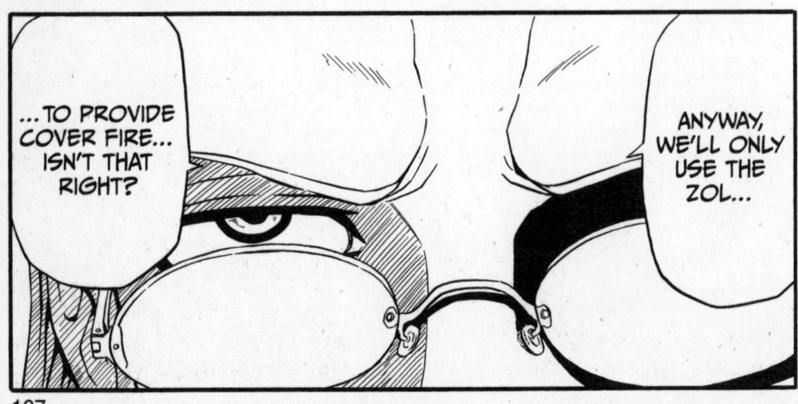
ANYWAY, WE'LL ONLY USE THE ZOL...
...TO PROVIDE COVER FIRE... ISN'T THAT RIGHT?

SHWOOOF
JIO, YOUR FRIEND, HAS NO KNOWL-EDGE OF THE THINGS I'VE DONE.
KILL ME, AND YOU KILL HIM. CAN YOU DO THAT?
WUP
AAH!
FWUM

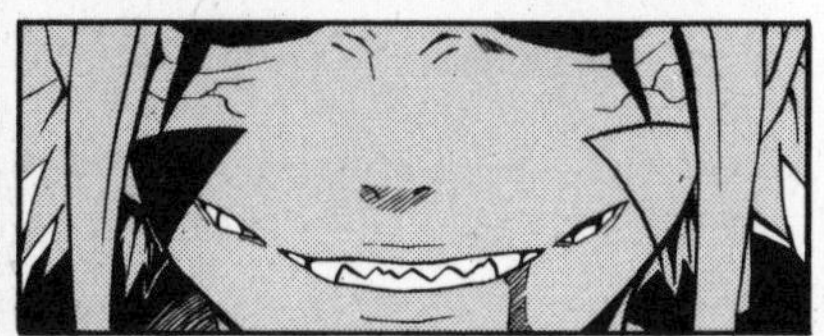
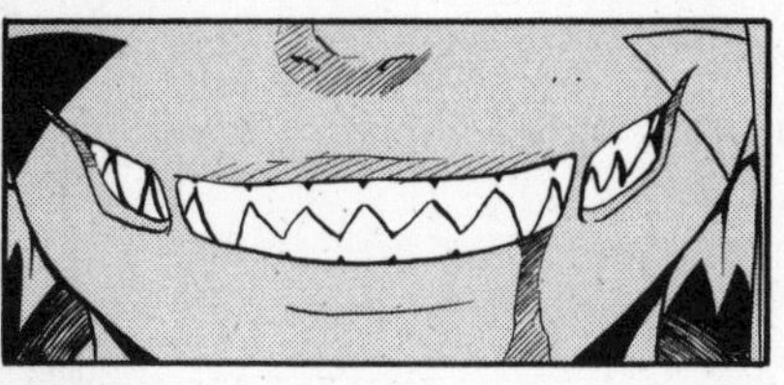

SO YOU'RE GOING TO KILL ME? HEH HEH...

I MUST DO IT...
SPLUP
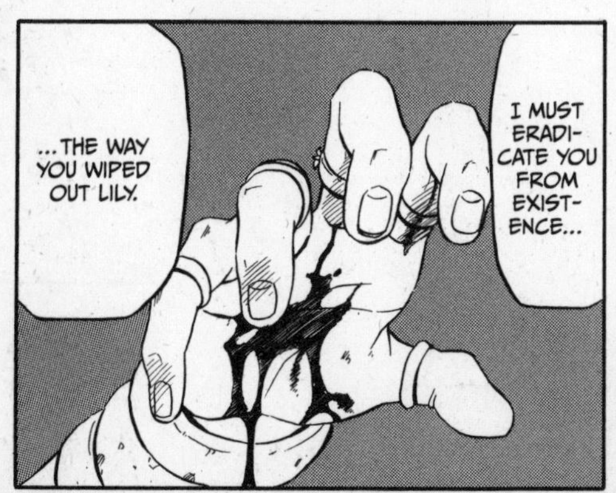
I MUST ERADICATE YOU FROM EXISTENCE...
...THE WAY YOU WIPED OUT LILY.

THAT'S WHY I'VE...
... I'VE ...

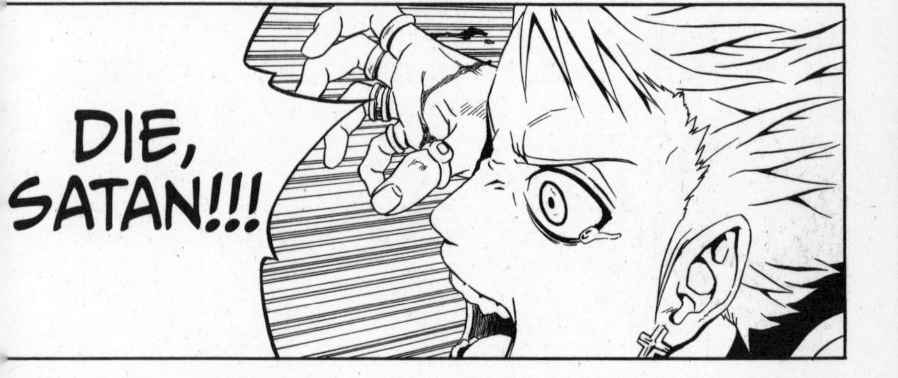
DIE, SATAN!!!

WIP
SWIK SWIK SWIK SWIK SWIK

KROOM

!

WIND!!

PWO OF

WHUP

WIND!!

PWOOF

FIRST O-PART.

SKLUSH
"ELEC-
TRIFIED
WATER.

AND
NOW...

WHISH

サンダードラゴン!!!
THUNDER DRAGON!!!

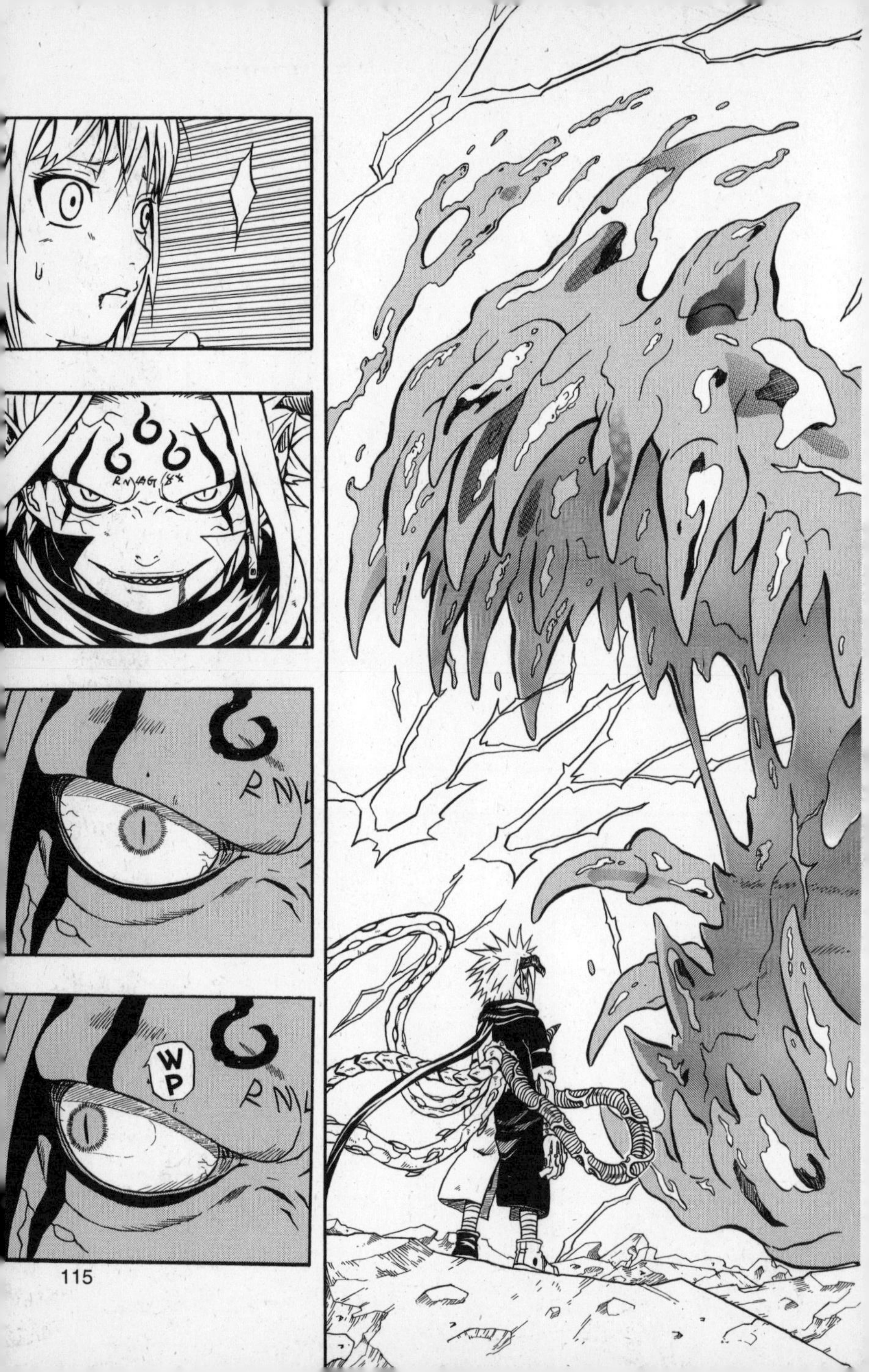
WP

KA WAM
KREEEN

HE BENT THUNDER DRAGON!!!
SKSSSH

SPUSH

SPZ
FASSSSH

STOP IT, CROSS! JIO WILL COME BACK, I PROMISE!
SHUT UP!!!

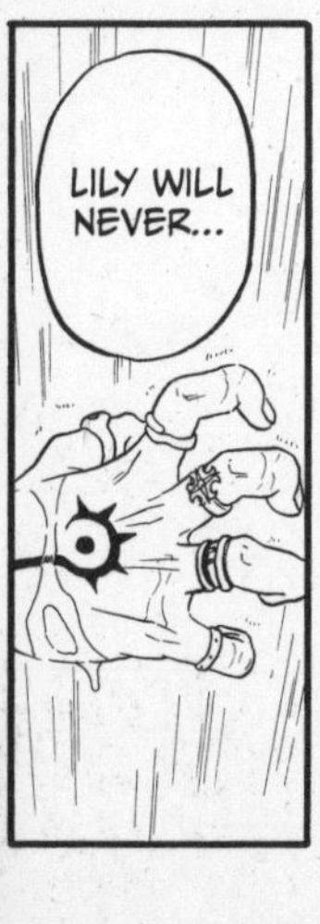
LILY WILL NEVER...

...COME BACK... NEVER!

MY MOM SAID HER PARENTS ABAN-DONED HER.
SHE'S TOO POOR TO AFFORD A DECENT MEAL.
WHERE DID YOU GET THOSE?
EVEN IN THAT TOUGH TIME SHE...
...STARTED SMILING AGAIN...
YOU STOLE THEM, DIDN'T YOU?
DIDN'T YOU?!
I JUST...
...I'M JUST A NUISANCE TO YOU...
YOU'LL LEAVE ME AND...
NEVER.
HUG
BUT... WHY...
WHY LILY?
WHY DID IT HAVE TO BE HER?!!
SATAN!! WHAT WILL IT TAKE TO SEND YOU BACK TO HELL?!!

DRIP

JUST... THE DIAMONDS IN THE ROUGH...

WHAT DO YOU MEAN?!

YOU ARE ONE SUCH DIAMOND, CROSS BIANCINA.
AND THE REASON LILY DIED IS BECAUSE...
...I WANTED TO PLUNGE YOUR UNIQUE POWERS INTO THE FORGE OF YOUR DARKEST PASSIONS.

MY... UNIQUE POWERS ...?

WHEN PURE GOOD IS TURNED TO THE DARK SIDE...
...IT CRE-ATES A MUCH PURER FORM OF HATRED.
SUCH HATRED IS FAR STRONGER AND DEADLIER THAN ANY OTHER KIND...

...AND I WILL TAKE IT FOR MY OWN, NOW THAT THE FORGE...

...HAS DONE ITS WORK...

HA HA HA...
...

...

WHO I AM...
...AND WHAT YOU WANT, AREN'T IMPORTANT.

WHEN LILY DIED, MY HEART DIED WITH HER.
I'M ALIVE RIGHT NOW BE-CAUSE...

...I VOWED TO KILL YOU, SATAN!!!

TAF

CRACK
EARTH.
CRACK

KRADOOM

CRASH

AAAH!

VOOP VOOP

SWUP
WHOA!
VOOSH

VENGEANCE MATTERS MORE TO YOU THAN ANYTHING...
A VENGEFUL SPIRIT THAT TRAN-SCENDS DEATH...

YOU WILL NEVER AWAKEN TO THE GOOD SIDE.
YES, YOU HAVE DEVELOPED WELL.

TOK
TOK

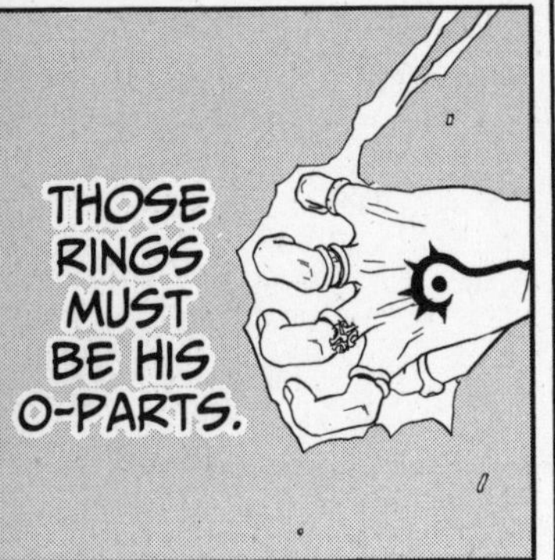
THOSE RINGS MUST BE HIS O-PARTS.

GLARE

TWITCH

KRRRIK
KRIIIK
!!

CRACK

VRRRM

ZOL IS CHARGING UP.

GLEEEAM

FIRE THE LASER...
...AT THE RED ALERT SIGNAL AT THE TOP OF ROCK BIRD... FULL POWER.

FULL POWER...
SHIN'S EFFECT, ZOL, IS A LASER THAT STRIPS AWAY SOULS. IF IT'S USED AT FULL POWER... WE MAY GET CAUGHT IN IT AS WELL...

VRRR

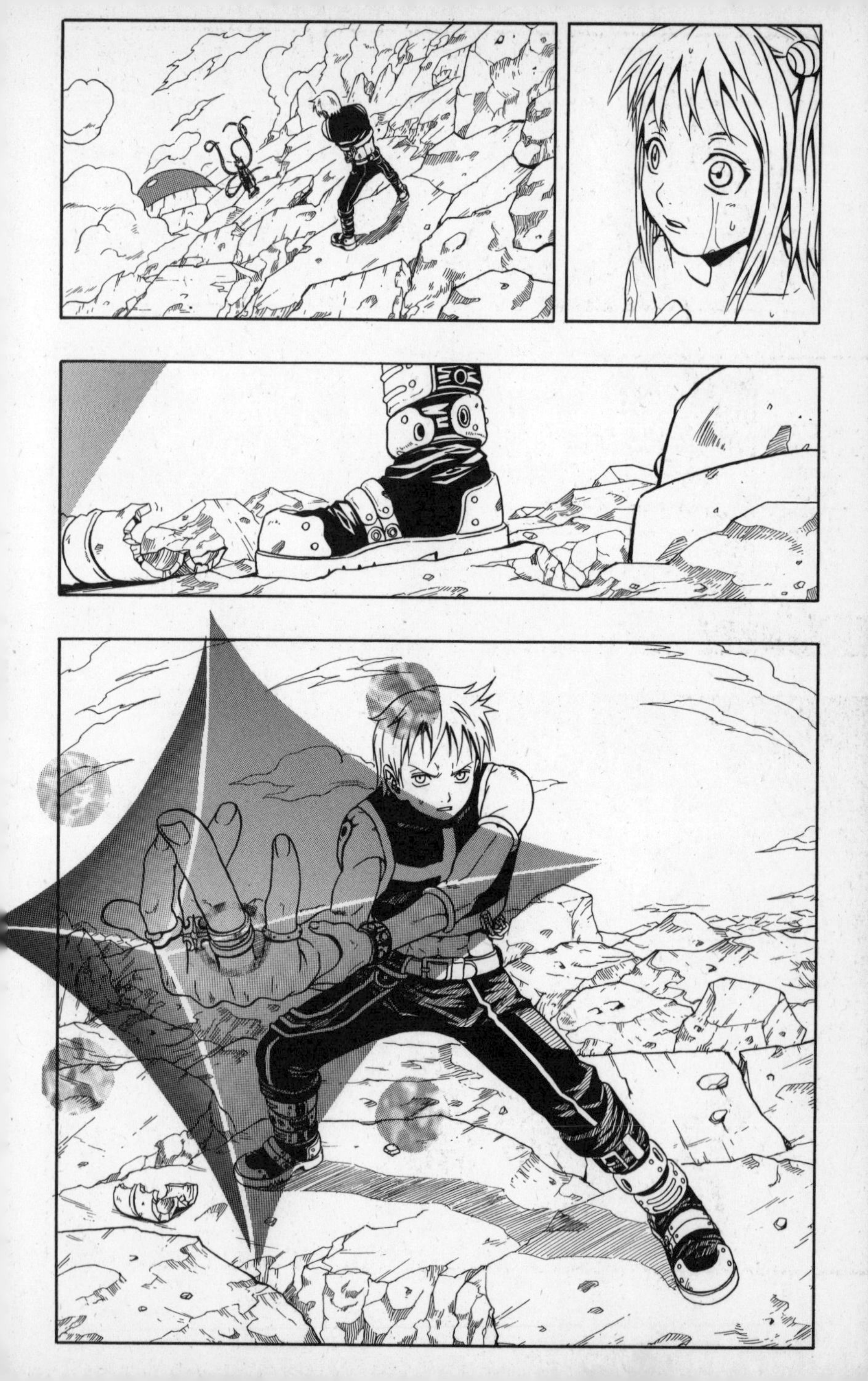

HMM... A FORCE FIELD EFFECT.
THAT'S WHAT PRO-TECTED HIM FROM MY EYE.

GRIN

CROSS IS REALLY SOME-THING.
BUT HIS EXPRES-SION, IT'S...

I LIKE YOUR EYES. IT'S ONLY A MATTER OF TIME BEFORE YOU'RE INFESTED WITH HATRED.
YOU'RE ONE STEP AWAY FROM TURNING TO THE DARK.

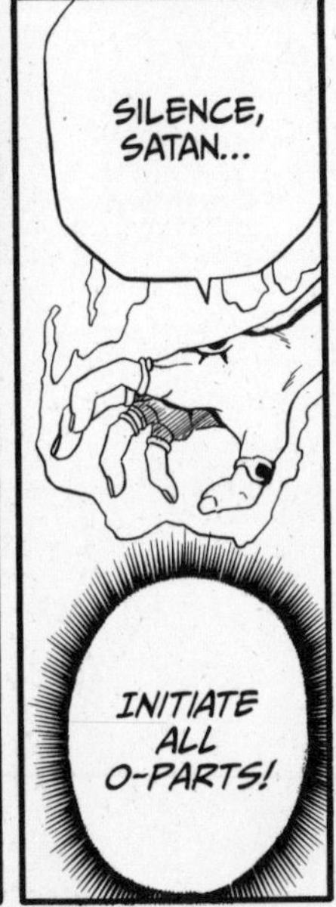
SILENCE, SATAN...
INITIATE ALL O-PARTS!

TIME TO FINISH YOU OFF.

五連ユニオン
ごれん
5 RING UNION...
DIE!

DIE!!
DASH

DIE!!!

HEH HEH HEH... THAT'S IT, ATTACK ME...
ATTACK ME IN HATRED! HOW PERFECT... FOR ME!

COME!
I WILL ABSORB YOU, AND YOU WILL BECOME A PART OF MY POWER.
DON'T DO THIS! YOU'LL BOTH DIE!
AAGH!
THWUMP
PLEASE... STOP...
STOP IT!
!

FLASH
WHAT ?!
UNNH...

LILY!!

LIGHT OF A PURE HEART...?

... EVERY-BODY'S ...
... HERO!

THANKS...
PLIP

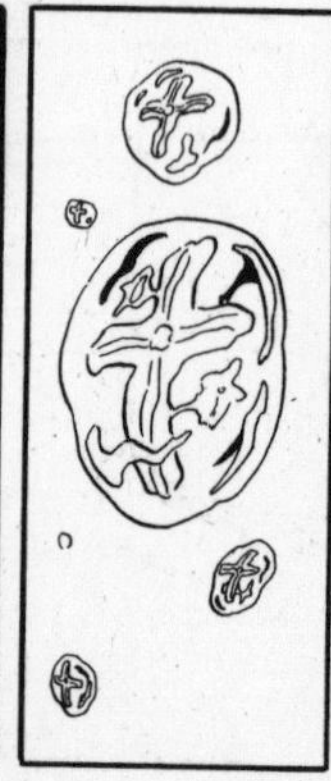

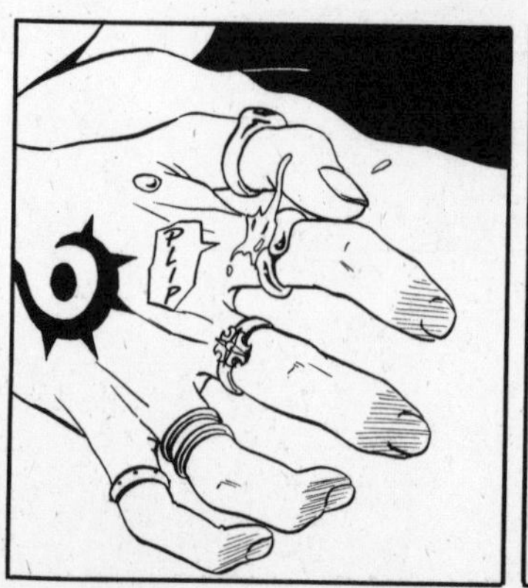

PLIP

ZHAAA!
AAAAH
WHAT IS THAT?
THE LIGHT ...
...IS GATH-ERING AROUND CROSS.

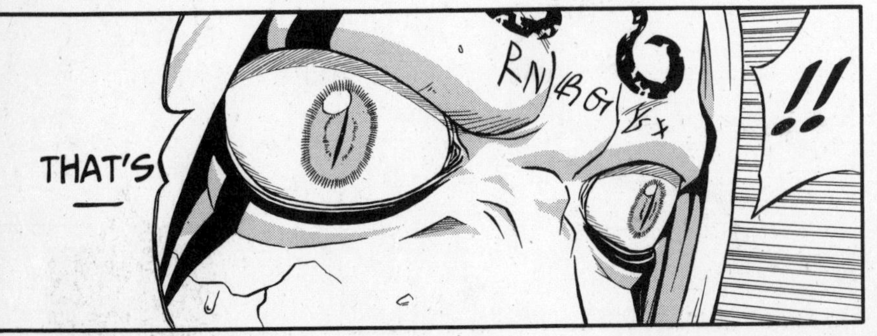
!!
THAT'S —

A SERAPH'S RING!!!
...LILY!
ZHEEN

BUT HOW?! NO WAY HIS SERAPH GENES COULD HAVE AWAKENED!!!

UH-OH... LOOKS LIKE REAL TROUBLE'S ARISING!

I DESTROYED HIS SISTER... WHO BACK THEN WAS THE KEY OF SOLOMON FOR THE FORMAL KABBALAH!!!

YET THE DARK I'D PLANTED INSIDE HIM HAS TURNED TO LIGHT!!
I CAN'T ABSORB HIM!!

GO!!
SHAAK

SPROING
THE LIGHT IS GIVING HIM STRENGTH.

YEOW! HIS RINGS!!
WOOSH

WIND!! DANCE OF THE GALE!
ELECTRI-FIED WATER!! THUNDER DRAGON!
EARTH!! EARTH IMPACT!
FIELD!! DEATH CAGE!
BOMB!! BLAST PUNCH!

FIVE RING...
LILY
BIANCINA!
5連リリィ・ビアンキーナ
FLASH

YOW!

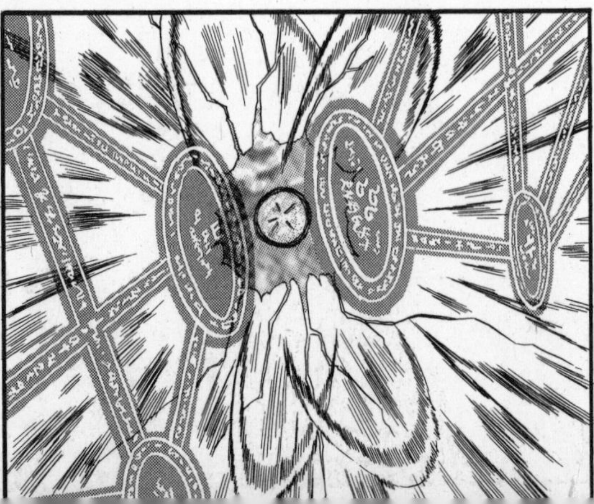

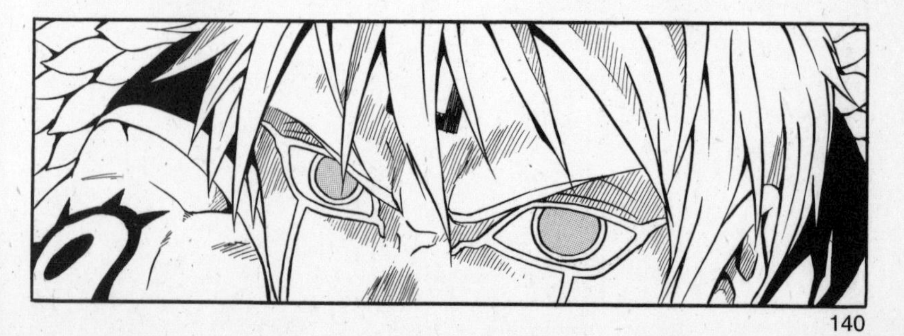

JIO...

THE LIGHT IS EATING INTO MY WOUND ...
I CAN'T REGEN-ERATE MY BODY...

CHAPTER 52
THE KEY OF SOLOMON

SHEEEN

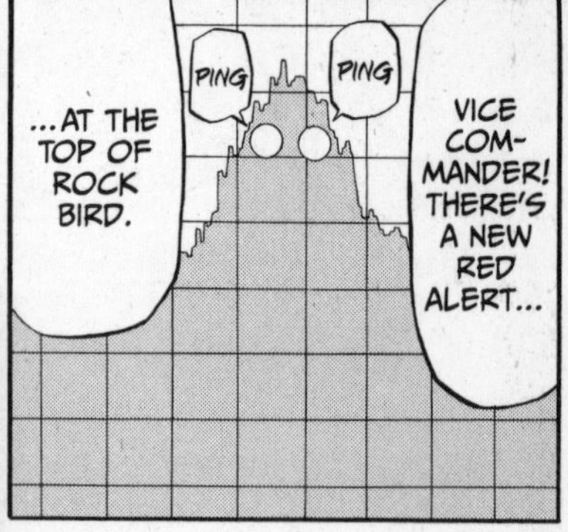
VICE COMMANDER! THERE'S A NEW RED ALERT...
PING
PING
...AT THE TOP OF ROCK BIRD.

!!
IS IT THAT BRAT CROSS ?!

...
THAT LIGHT... WHAT'S GOING ON UP THERE?

OR MAYBE IT'S THAT OLD HAG WHO ASSIGNED CROSS TO SHIN...
AMATERASU MIKO, THE PHANTOM, LEADER OF THE STEA GOVERNMENT... ARE *YOU* BEHIND THIS?

VICE COMMANDER!!

ZOL'S CHARGED UP TO 85 PERCENT!
ONCE WE LOCK ONTO THE TARGET IT SHOULD BE AT 100 PERCENT!!

A COUNTRY WITH AN AGED LEADER WHO WON'T RETIRE WON'T LAST LONG.
TIP

DRIP
PLIP

THE ONLY REASON I'VE WORKED UNDER MISHIMA AND CROSS IS SO I CAN BECOME COMMANDER OF SHIN...

LOCK-ON
COMPLETE.

GLARE

SHEEEEN

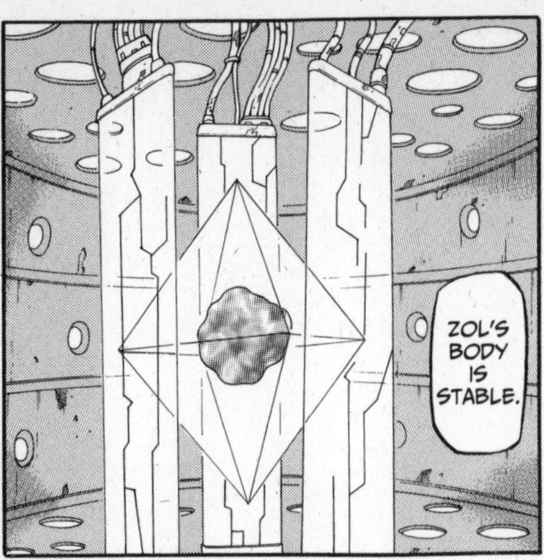
ZOL'S BODY IS STABLE.

...AND DECLARE IT AN INDEPENDENT STATE, ENABLING ME TO TAKE THE KABBALAH FROM THE STEA GOVERNMENT.
SP

AND THEN... I WILL RULE THE WORLD!
VRR
KRK

STEA GOVERNMENT HEADQUARTERS

BLUB
BLUB

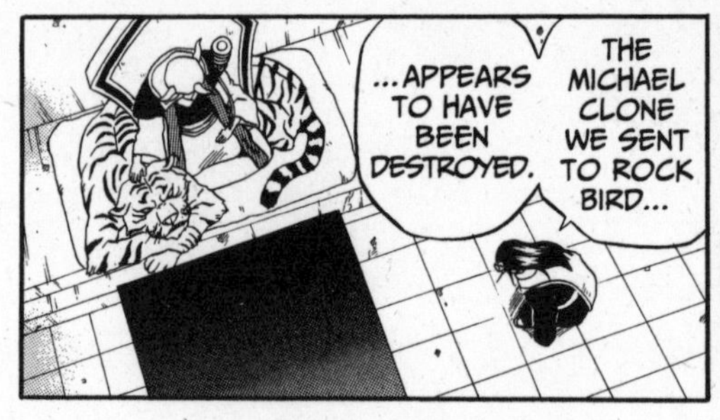
THE MICHAEL CLONE WE SENT TO ROCK BIRD...
...APPEARS TO HAVE BEEN DESTROYED.

I WILL ACCEPT ANY PENALTY ...
...FOR ALLOWING THE FAILURE OF THIS PLAN, MILADY.

IF I'D BEEN IN CHARGE, IT WOULDN'T HAVE TURNED OUT LIKE THIS.
A YOUNGSTER LIKE YOU JUST ISN'T ABLE TO MEET HER DEMANDS AND EXPECTATIONS.

CROSS-SCARRED DOFWA
CHIEF OF STAFF

AMATERASU MIKO, THE PHANTOM
LEADER OF THE STEA GOVERNMENT

KRU MP
TMPH

THWUMP
FL AP
SWUH

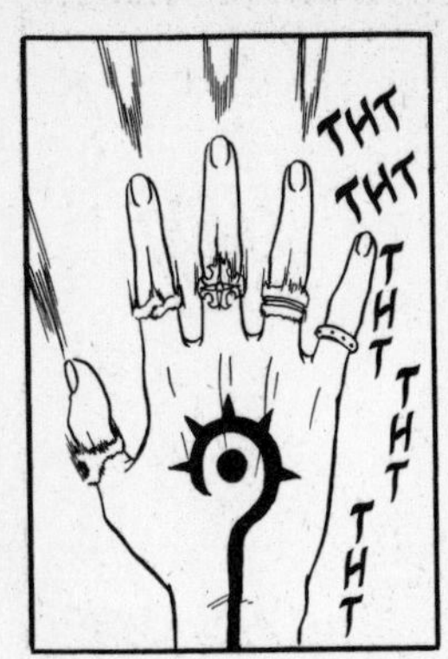
THT
THT
THT
THT
THT
THT

CROSS IS...

...AN ANGEL?!

SO THIS SECRET OF YOURS ...

...WAS THAT BOY?
CROSS BIANCINA, COMMANDER IN CHIEF OF SHIN?!

TELL ME, HOW MANY RECIPES DO WE...
...THE STEA GOVERNMENT, ACTUALLY KNOW ABOUT?

YOU KNOW AS WELL AS I THAT SUCH A RECIPE AS CROSS...
...CANNOT BE INSTALLED INTO THE KABBALAH...
...UNTIL IT IS AWAKENED.

AND JUST EXACTLY HOW ARE THEY AWAKENED?

PROXIMITY TO *IT* IS ESSENTIAL.
MISHIMA KNOWS ABOUT THIS TOO?!

SO... WHAT IS THIS THING ?!
WHAT IS "IT"?!

IT IS...

THE KEY OF SOLOMON.

WHY?!!
YOU SHOULD NEVER HAVE AWAKENED AS AN ANGEL!!!

...

THE KEY OF SOLO-MON... FOR THE ANGELS...
...SHOULD'VE BEEN DESTROYED WITH LILY!!!

LILY... THE KEY OF SOL-OMON...?
WHAT ARE YOU TALKING ABOUT?!!

IS THAT IT?!
IS THAT THE REASON YOU KILLED LILY?!!

YES! THE *KEY OF SOLOMON* AWAKENS A DIAMOND IN THE ROUGH INTO A RECIPE.
(AWAK-ENING)
NEED
CROSS DIAMOND IN THE ROUGH
CROSS ANGEL
LILY THE KEY OF SOLOMON

THAT'S WHAT YOUR SISTER LILY WAS.

WITHOUT LILY, THERE WAS NO CHANCE YOU COULD AWAKEN AS AN ANGEL...
SO I WAS GOING TO DRAG YOU DOWN TO MY SIDE.

BUT I CAN'T ABSORB YOU NOW THAT YOU'RE AN ANGEL.
BELIEVE ALL THAT OR NOT, AS YOU LIKE.

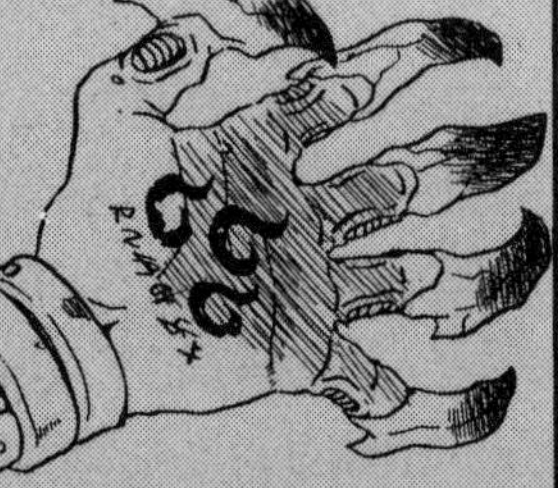

IF WHAT YOU SAY IS TRUE, WHO WAS LILY... WHO ARE WE?
IT CAN'T BE COINCI-DENCE, CAN IT?!

THIRTEEN YEARS AGO WE TRACKED DOWN RECIPE NUMBER ONE, METATRON, FOR THE FORMAL KABBALAH.
BUT LIKE ANGEL NUMBER 10, SANDALPHON, WHICH WE'D ALREADY FOUND...

...IT WAS AN UNAWAKENED DIAMOND IN THE ROUGH THAT HAD TAKEN HUMAN FORM.
THIS FORM WAS A BOY ABOUT TWO YEARS OLD, AND WE NAMED HIM CROSS.

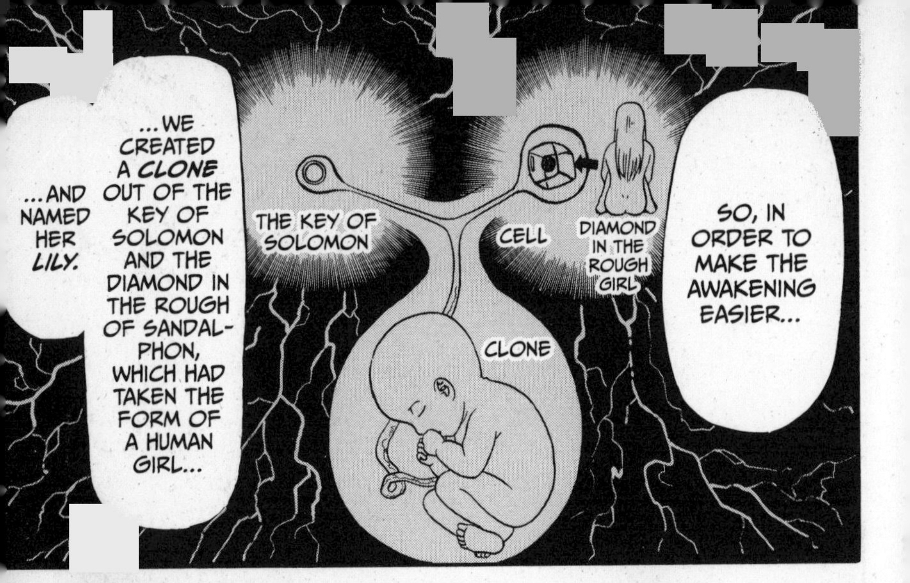
SO, IN ORDER TO MAKE THE AWAKENING EASIER...
DIAMOND IN THE ROUGH GIRL
CELL
THE KEY OF SOLOMON
CLONE
...WE CREATED A *CLONE* OUT OF THE KEY OF SOLOMON AND THE DIAMOND IN THE ROUGH OF SANDALPHON, WHICH HAD TAKEN THE FORM OF A HUMAN GIRL...
...AND NAMED HER *LILY.*

AND PLACED HER WITH CROSS WHILE HE WAS STILL YOUNG.

I HAD THEM LIVE IN A SMALL VILLAGE WITH A CHURCH...

...ASSIGNING TWO OF OUR AGENTS TO POSE AS THEIR PARENTS...
...TO KEEP WATCH OVER THEM WHILE THEY GREW UP.

BUT YEARS PASSED, AND CROSS DIDN'T AWAKEN...

...SO, TO CHANGE THE SCENARIO, I HAD THE AGENTS LEAVE THE VILLAGE...
...LEAVING CROSS AND LILY TO FEND FOR THEM-SELVES.

A WHILE LATER, THAT *INCIDENT* OCCURRED...
...AND THE CLONE OF THE KEY DIED.

THE DRAGON'S EYE INCIDENT!!

THAT'S WHY I TOOK CROSS ON...
...AS COMMANDER IN CHIEF OF SHIN, EVEN THOUGH HE WAS STILL VERY YOUNG.

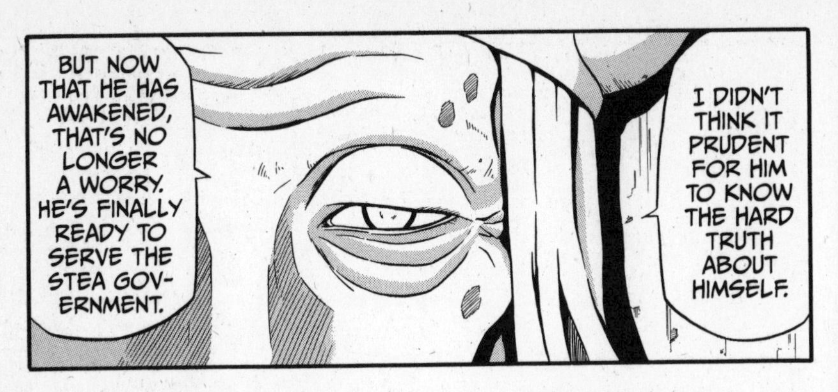
I DIDN'T THINK IT PRUDENT FOR HIM TO KNOW THE HARD TRUTH ABOUT HIMSELF.
BUT NOW THAT HE HAS AWAKENED, THAT'S NO LONGER A WORRY. HE'S FINALLY READY TO SERVE THE STEA GOV-ERNMENT.

BUT IF THE CLONE FOR THE KEY IS DEAD...
...WHAT CAUSED CROSS TO AWAKEN?
FATE, PER-HAPS...

YOU SEE, WHEN WE CREATED LILY, A TRAITOR IN OUR MIDST...
...STOLE AWAY WITH THE ORIGINAL KEY OF SOLOMON AND THE SANDALPHON GIRL...

WHO... WHO WAS THIS TRAITOR?

IT WAS...

...THE FORMER CAPTAIN OF THE STEA GOVERNMENT ARMY'S FIRST ATTACK SQUAD...
...ZECT CRESCENT, THE RED WIND.

THE RED WIND?! UNBELIEVABLE!

I'D HEARD THAT HE'D DISAPPEARED, BUT I NEVER THOUGHT HE'D HAVE DONE SUCH A THING.

ZECT TREATED SANDALPHON, IN HUMAN FORM, AS IF SHE WAS HIS OWN CHILD...

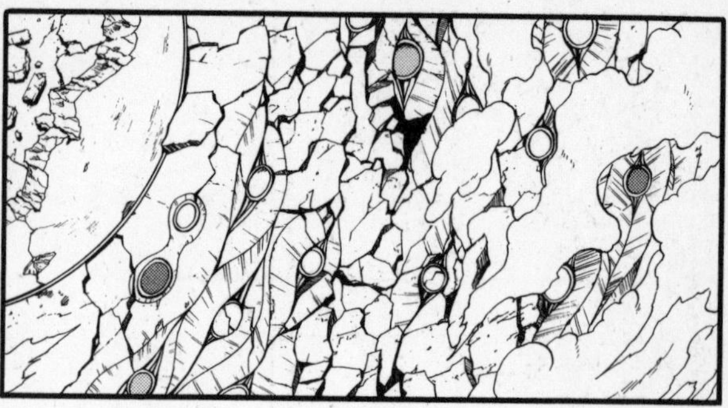

DASH

JIO!!!

CROSS!! HOW COULD YOU DO THIS TO HIM?!

YOU KNOW IT WASN'T JIO I WAS FIGHTING, RUBY...

...IT WAS SATAN!

...

HMPH!

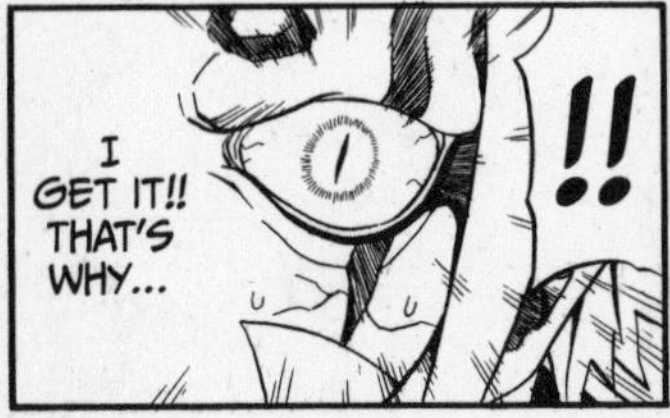
!!
I GET IT!! THAT'S WHY...

FLASH
?!

ZHEEN

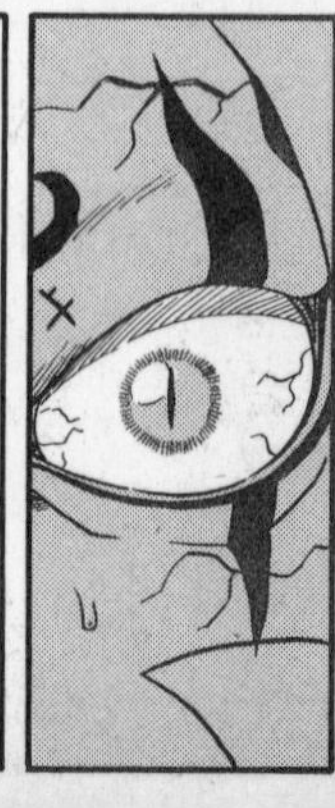

THAT PENDANT ...
IS IT THE ORIGINAL KEY OF SOLOMON ?!!

NO! IT CAN'T BE!!

LILY TAUGHT ME TO...

SATAN... I'M GOING TO BRING JUSTICE UPON YOU...
...BUT IT WILL BE WITH A PURE HEART, FREE OF HATRED.

PREPARE TO DIE!!
SWUH

I KNOW I MUSTN'T HELP SATAN, BUT...

CROSS !!
GOODBYE.
FLAP

WH ISH
VOOSH
CROSS! DON'T!!
SWUFF

?!
AAAH!

SHEE

HAH
HOW DO YOU LIKE THAT, MY TWO DEAR RECIPES ?!
IT'S ZOL, AT FULL POWER.

DAMN IT, THIS IS SUICIDAL!
AT THIS LEVEL, ZOL COULD STRIP US ALL OF OUR SOULS!

HEY! ZOL'S FIRING!
AT FULL POWER! WHY WEREN'T WE ALERTED?!
WOW!

GWOM
ZOL'S REALLY FRYING THE SKY!!
I'VE NEVER SEEN IT CRANKED UP LIKE THIS!!

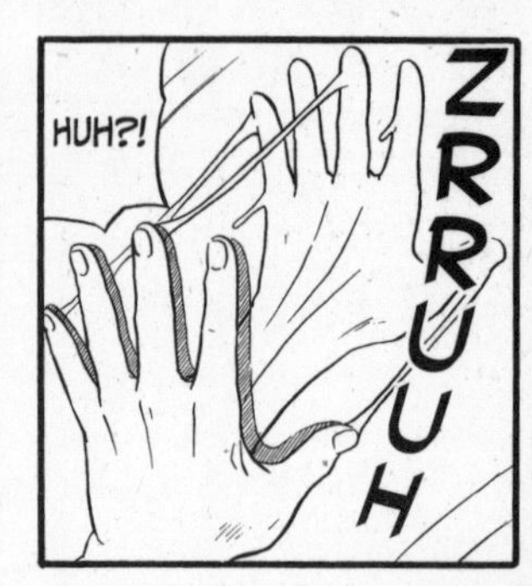
ZRRUUH
HUH?!

ZRRRUUUUH
HEY, WAIT... WAIT A MINUTE! WHAT'S HAP-PENING TO ME?!!

AGH! MY BODY!!
NO! I DON'T WANT TO DIE YET!!
CLONK

NRRUUUUH
AAARGH!
YAAAH!
THWUMP

AAAH! I'M BEING PULLED TO ZOL'S BEAM!!
AAH!
GAARGH!
AAAH!

AAAH...
EEEEE...
AAAI...

KA-WHAM
(sound effect, printed with the K and W on the left and the A and M on the right)

WHA... WHAT'S GOING ON?!
ZRRRUUUH
(sound effect, printed top to bottom)

CRRRRACK
AAH!

SO THIS WAS YOUR PLAN, BALSA...
SHIELD

...TO ELIMINATE ME AND SATAN AT ONE GO.
BUT USING THE ZOL LIKE THIS... IT'S INSANE!!

I CAN'T BELIEVE I HAVE TO SHIELD MYSELF LIKE THIS!
BUT WHAT'S WORSE IS I CAN'T REGEN-ERATE MY BODY WITH ANGEL'S LIGHT EATING INTO IT! AT THIS RATE, I'LL...

!!

HUH?!
ZRUH
ZRRUUUH
SLUMP
YOU'VE KEPT YOURSELF WELL HIDDEN.
I THOUGHT YOU WERE JUST AN ORDINARY HUMAN, BUT...
THAT'S RIGHT !!

HEH HEH HEH ...
HEH HEH ...

HA HA HA HA HA!

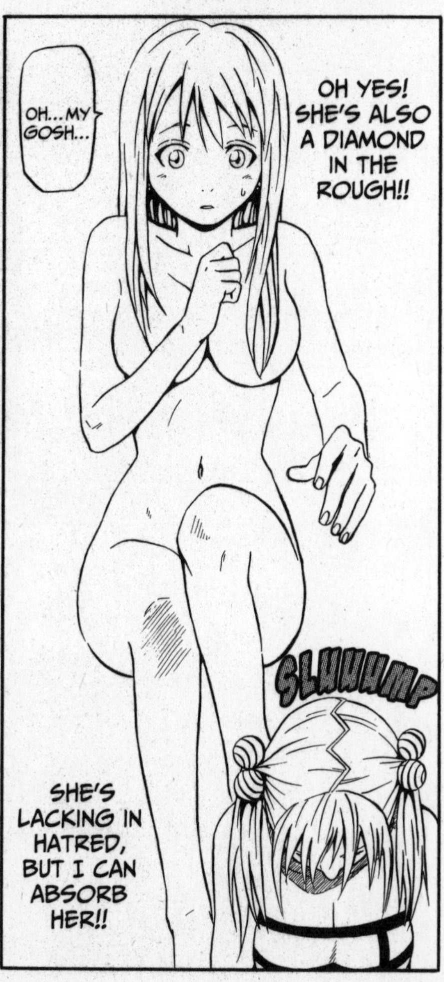
OH YES! SHE'S ALSO A DIAMOND IN THE ROUGH!!
OH... MY GOSH...
SLUUUMP
SHE'S LACKING IN HATRED, BUT I CAN ABSORB HER!!

THAT SHOULD GIVE ME THE POWER TO HEAL THESE WOUNDS.
SUH

HER SOUL'S BEEN STRIPPED AWAY BY THE ZOL!
SHE'S GOING TO...
...

EH?
YEEEEK! I'M NAKED!!
THERE'D BETTER BE A GOOD EXPLANATION FOR THIS!

THAT'S NOT IMPORTANT, RUBY!
YOU'RE ALREADY HALF-DEAD!!
BUT...

YEEEEK! I'M NAKED!!
AVERT YOUR EYES, YOU COSMIC PERVERTS!!!

RUBY! IF YOU WANT JIO'S BODY TO HEAL...
...YOU MUST LET ME ABSORB YOU!!
UH...

WSS
SHOOOM
...

DAMN IT!!

CROSS, DON'T TRY TO...
...STOP ME.

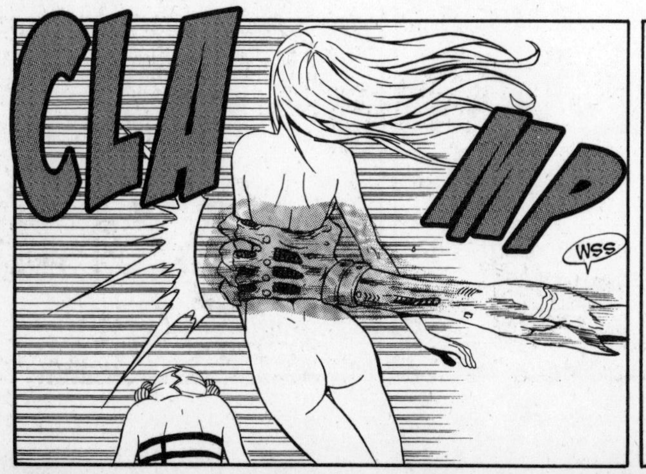
CLAMP
WSS

DON'T! I THOUGHT YOU UNDER-STOOD HE'S *SATAN*, NOT JIO!!
HE'S ONLY GOING TO USE YOU!!!

I'M SORRY, CROSS... BUT I...
...I MUST SEE JIO AGAIN...

GRIN

YOU'D SELL YOUR SOUL FOR A COMMON DESIRE?!!

I HAVE FAITH, CROSS! I BE-LIEVE...
...JIO'S HEART IS STILL IN THERE SOME-WHERE!!

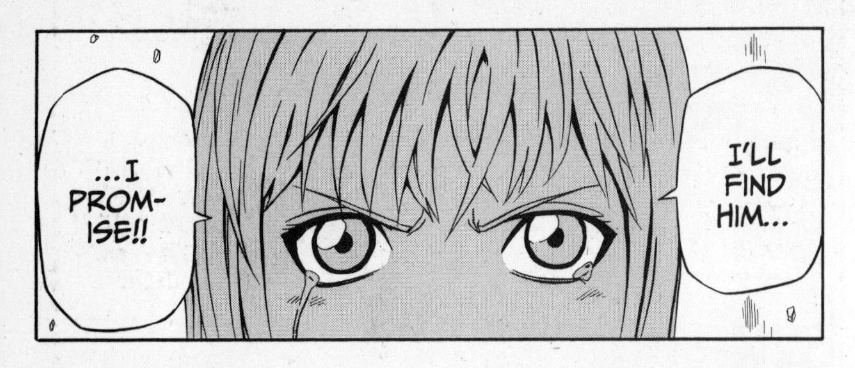
I'LL FIND HIM...
...I PROM-ISE!!

EVEN SO, THERE'S NO KNOWING IF JIO WILL COME BACK!!
EITHER WAY, SATAN WILL STILL HAVE YOU!!!

ABSORB!!!

FZZSSH

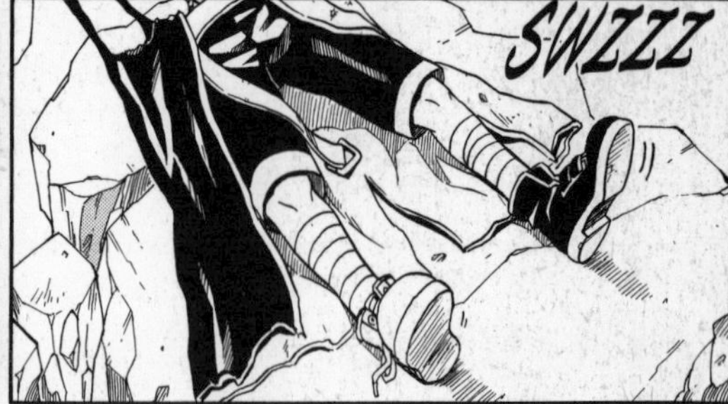
SWZZZ

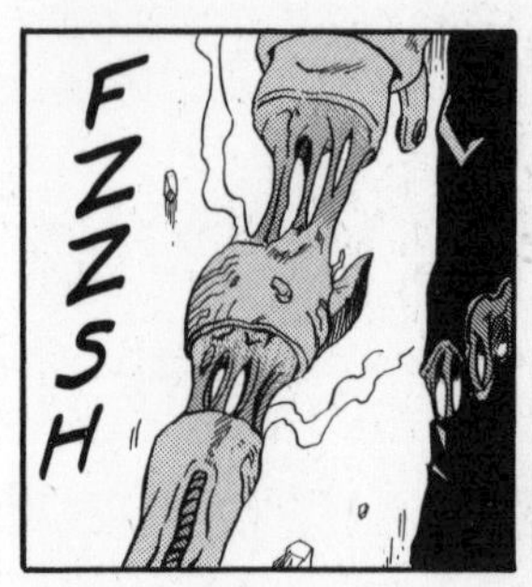
FZZZSH

SWUU

BLINK

DARK... COLD... I MUST BE INSIDE SATAN...

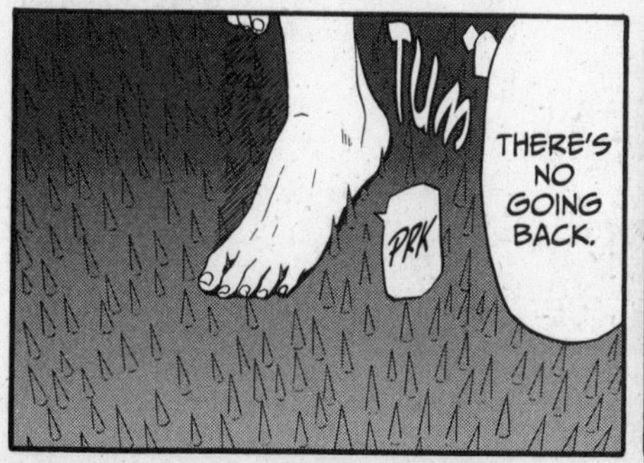
TUM
THERE'S NO GOING BACK.
PRK

STARE

OUCH!

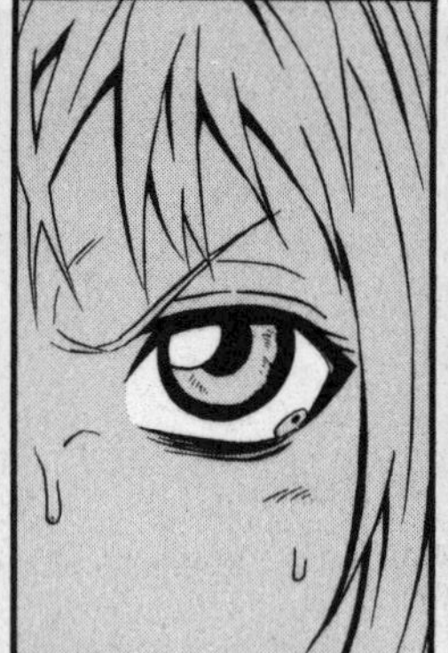

SHUH
JIO...
SPLUB

PANT
SKCH
I'LL FIND YOU, JIO... I WILL!
PANT

AND I'LL SAVE YOU!!
SKCH

JUST HOLD ON!!!

YOUR LIGHT WON'T BE TROUBLING ME ANYMORE.
SHALL WE CON- TINUE?

I CAN'T DO ANYTHING... OR MAYBE I'M JUST NOT TRYING...
SO WHAT IF I TAKE A BREAK?
I'VE BEEN FIGHTING SATAN ALL THIS TIME...
DON'T I AT LEAST GET CREDIT FOR THAT?

MAYBE I'M SO DOWN ON MYSELF BECAUSE I'M ALONE...
I NEVER THOUGHT I WAS SO WEAK...

YOU FINALLY NOTICED, EH?
TOOK YOU LONG ENOUGH!

HUH?

THAT'S WHY YOU'VE GOT FRIENDS, Y'KNOW.
NICE TO SEE YOU AGAIN.
DAH
DUM
WOBBLE
WOBBLE
YOW!

B-BMP B-BMP
RUBY?! WHAT'RE YOU DOING HERE...
...LIKE THAT... AND ALL CUT UP AND BRUISED AND...

IT'S A LONG STORY I WON'T...
...WASTE TIME ON RIGHT NOW.

JUST CLOSE YOUR EYES AND REACH OUT YOUR HAND.
No peeking!
OH... UH... RIGHT!!
UNN
SWUH

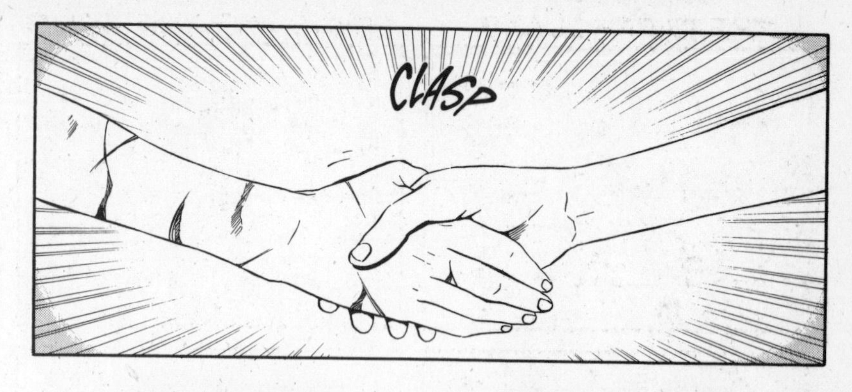
CLASP

HUH?
BLUSH

YOU NEED TO TRUST ME, JIO.
DON'T LET GO OF MY HAND.
TUG

NOW, LET'S GET OUT OF THIS DARKNESS!

SEISHI AND THE SONG

SEISHI AND THE EARTHQUAKE

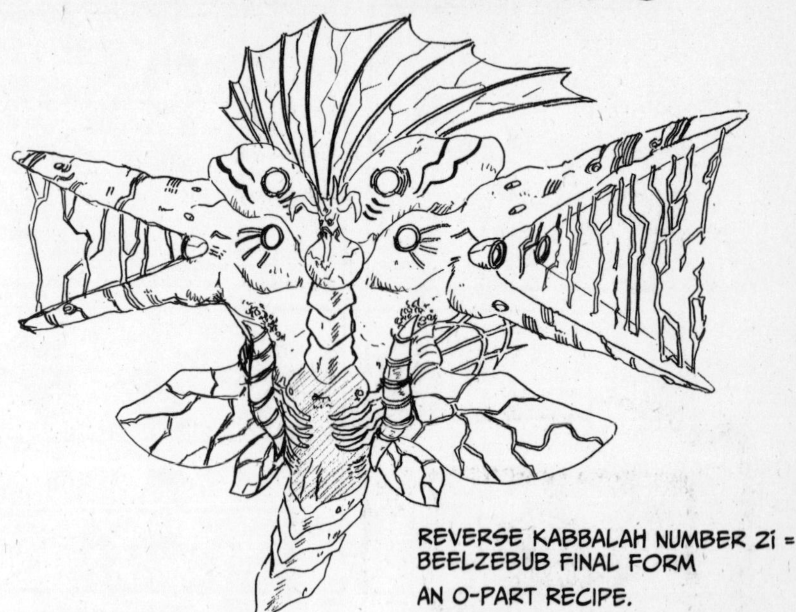

REVERSE KABBALAH NUMBER 21 = BEELZEBUB FINAL FORM

AN O-PART RECIPE.

THIS IS BEELZEBUB'S TRUE FORM AS IT APPEARS IN MYTHS AND LEGENDS. WITH HIS WINGS HE'S ABLE TO CAUSE HUGE TSUNAMIS AND CREATE HIS OWN ELECTROMAGNETIC FIELD. HE'S SO HUGE THAT IT'S PRETTY MUCH IMPOSSIBLE TO ESCAPE FROM HIM.

REVERSE KABBALAH NUMBER 21 = BEELZEBUB SECOND FORM

AN O-PART RECIPE.

BEELZEBUB'S SECOND FORM, WHICH ENABLES HIM TO MAKE FULL USE OF FRAP MIND, A METHOD OF CONTROLLING THE MOVEMENTS OF OTHERS.

THE KEY OF SOLOMON (RUBY'S PENDANT)

THIS IS WHAT AWAKENS A DIAMOND IN THE ROUGH BEFORE HE OR SHE BECOMES A RECIPE (ANGEL, DEMON). THERE MAY BE OTHER SUCH KEYS THAT CAN ALSO AWAKEN A RECIPE... JUST LIKE LILY...

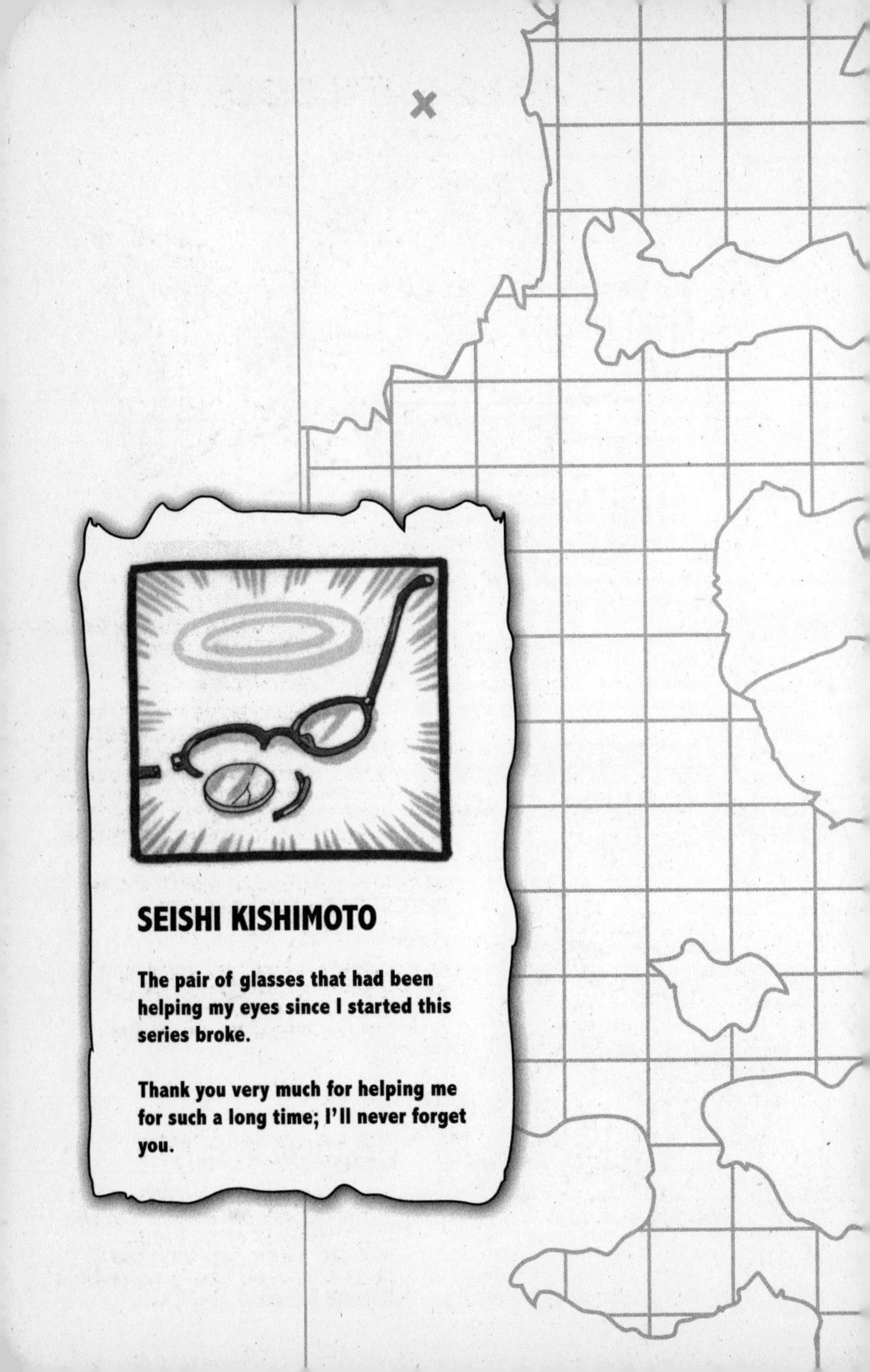

SEISHI KISHIMOTO

The pair of glasses that had been helping my eyes since I started this series broke.

Thank you very much for helping me for such a long time; I'll never forget you.

VIZ Media Edition
STORY AND ART BY SEISHI KISHIMOTO

English Adaptation/David R. Valois
Translation/Tetsuichiro Miyaki
Touch-up Art & Lettering/HudsonYards
Design/Andrea Rice
Editor/Gary Leach

Editor in Chief, Books/Alvin Lu
Editor in Chief, Magazines/Marc Weidenbaum
VP, Publishing Licensing/Rika Inouye
VP, Sales & Product Marketing/Gonzalo Ferreyra
VP, Creative/Linda Espinosa
Publisher/Hyoe Narita

Printed in the U.S.A.

Published by VIZ Media, LLC
P.O. Box 77010
San Francisco, CA 94107

10 9 8 7 6 5 4 3 2 1
First printing, December 2008

www.viz.com

store.viz.com

PARENTAL ADVISORY
O-PARTS HUNTER is rated T+ for Older Teen and is recommended for ages 16 and up. This volume contains realistic and fantasy violence and adult situations.

ratings.viz.com